Deena Stryker

A TAOIST POLITICS
The Case for Sacredness

Deena Stryker is an independent journalist and author who holds dual US and French citizenship. She has lived and worked in half a dozen countries on both sides of the former Iron Curtain, taught future studies at the University of Massachusetts and written speeches in the Carter State Department. She lives in Philadelphia, is a senior editor at OpedNews.com. and blogs at www.otherjonesii.blogspot.com.

The Two Hundred Days of "8 1/2" (as Deena Boyer) The day by day account of the making of the Fellini film '8 1/2'

Cuba 1964: When the Revolution Was Young includes candid conversations with the members of the five year old Cuban government showing they did not embrace communism until well after the revolution. Her Cuba photo archive is available on-line at Duke University.

Une autre Europe, un autre Monde (in French) foresaw the reunification of Europe and the dissolution of the Soviet Union.

Lunch with Fellini, Dinner with Fidel: A Journey from the Cold War to the Arab Spring, a memoir

America Revealed to a Honey-Colored World, a pamphlet focusing on key periods in U.S. history.

Lovers and Others: Short Stories and Vignettes

Everything that makes diversity of kinds, species, differences, properties, everything which depends on generation, corruption, alienation and change is not being or existence, but is a condition and circumstance of being or existence which is one, infinite, immobile, subject, matter, life, soul, truth and good.
Giordano Bruno, 1548-1600

A religion, old or new, that stressed the magnificence of the universe as revealed by modern science might be able to draw forth reserves of reverence and awe hardly tapped by the conventional faiths. Sooner or later, such a religion will emerge
Carl Sagan, 1934-1996

Some readers I know will take particular exception to the term "sacred" because it will suggest to them that the conviction I have in mind is necessarily a theistic one. I shall try to explain why it is not, and how it may be, and commonly is, interpreted in a secular as well as a conventionally religious way.
Ronald Dworkin, 1931-20

TABLE OF CONTENTS

Preface

On September 11th, 2001, Americans discovered that many people in the world hate us, either because we are not religious enough, seeking to foist our materialist culture on them, or because we are reluctant to share our wealth. As Washington continues the imperialist policies that gave rise to terrorism, protests and uprisings motivated by religious zeal and calls for political change continue unabated.

This book should help those on all sides of the debate to see things in terms other than right and wrong. In the writing long before the catastrophe that changed America overnight, it uses circular, or systems thinking, the new physics and the new biology, to arrive at three basic notions: internal authority, sacredness and order/disorder. Taken together, they could allow us to move from God-based religion to a spirituality that restores responsibility to the exercise of freedom.

From the early seventies until the present, my own freedom has been to think about politics and the world while raising two children, marrying, divorcing and moving from one country, culture and language to several others. In the eighties I wrote a book in French that drew attention to a fundamental difference between the European and American versions of democracy, in order to persuade Europeans that they had an independent role to play in the standoff with the Soviet Union. Rejected by every major publisher in France, it foresaw the reunification of Europe and the dissolution of the Soviet Union. An independent publisher handed me the first copies on the day the Berlin Wall fell.

Perhaps because the fall of the Wall had made the slogan 'Better Dead than Red' obsolete, perhaps because I was losing a friend to cancer, the systems thinking that had enabled me to foresee the reunification of Europe now led me to consider attitudes toward death. Although I had been an agnostic since the age of ten, from there it was inevitable that I confront religion. Very quickly, a childhood math block was replaced by the thrilling discovery that, unlike religion, physics and biology had *meaning*! Reading Heisenberg and Bohm, and the more user-friendly Capra and Zukav, it occured to me that their findings could help resolve not only ecological but also political challenges.

I remembered that although Einstein was not religiously inclined, he believed that creation had been a rational process, and hoped to find an equation that would account for it. Seeing that the world was subject instead to "an insidious cancer of randomness and probabilities," he famously cried out: "God doesn't play dice!" If even Einstein could believe in what today is called the design theory of evolution, it is not surprising that most people relate to the world from a religious perspective. In America, church-goers represent a larger percentage than in other highly developed nations, yet since 9/11 our search for meaning has become desperate and we wonder why the rest of the world does not see us as a people committed to the good.

In his recent *From the Ruins of Empire*, the Indian historian Pankaj Mishra ascribes nineteenth century Oriental resentment of Western imperialism and racism in large part to the non-dual nature of its religions. That resentment has gradually permeated the entire developing world, inspiring uprisings that meld the spiritual and the political.

In *The Human Web*, published in 2003, the historians J.R. and William McNeill apply systems thinking to the past. Here we shall consider the future in terms of the systems we inherit and create, and which are ruled as much by chance and necessity as by rationality. With the help of ancient and modern thinkers, we'll combine the Hindu *tat tvam asi*, that art thou, with the insights of the Blakes, Brunos and Lennons who say: "I have seen the world and to it I belong."

I
The Problématique

*The good life of the good person can
only be fully realized in the good society.
Prosperity can only be conceived as a
condition that includes obligations and
responsibilities to others.*
Zia Zardar

After the fall of the Berlin Wall in 1989, there
was a gradual dimming of the foreign policy debate
until, by the end of the century, the main players in the
Cold War had become cautious partners. The task of
achieving a peaceful existence for the exponentially
growing world population was seen exclusively in material terms until, in the developed world (henceforth
'the North'), global warming challenged the belief in
progress and freedom, just as large parts of the developing world, (or 'South') was falling prey to Islamic
extremism, and anti-globalization movements took
hold across the globe.

Globalization marks the epitome of what I call
external authority, in which a minority exercises
power over a majority. Neo-liberal external authority
secured its position by anointing external freedom as
an absolute, obscuring the internal freedom that powers individual, or internal authority. The case for sacredness that I will make here is not about religion but
about responsibility. It will contrast the linear thinking

that created a privileged place for unlimited freedom to act, to the circular thinking found in ancient civilizations as well as in modern science, and which, by revealing external freedom's limits, provides a new foundation for morality.

The problems of the 21st century are often referred to as 'the problématique', a term coined in the sixties by a hundred industrialists, thinkers and researchers from around the world gathered in the Club of Rome, to designate major issues that need to be considered together in order to be resolved. Ahead of their time, these people understood that the problems of food, population, pollution, resources, and weapons of mass destruction could not be dealt with separately, and that it was urgent to study their interactions. Recognizing that the earth is a system, in which the modification of one part modifies the whole, they financed models of the world based on the new science of systems analysis.

The first Report to the Club of Rome, Dennis and Donella Meadows' *The Limits to Growth*, landed like a bombshell in the capitals of the Western world in 1972, only to be swiftly ejected by the media under the derogatory label of 'doomsday approach'. Subsequent research teams funded by the Club of Rome each took a different approach to the problématique, however their reports had less of an impact than the first, probably because in the seventies and eighties, nothing could match the threat of potential annihilation inherent in the U.S.-Soviet antagonism.

With the end of the East/West conflict, the nuclear threat receded, however it continues to loom in Iran's determination to harness nuclear energy for peaceful purposes, as well as in North Korea's insistence on arming itself against perceived threats from the United States. And while the South is engaged in an extraordinary number of violent conflicts, the North is disintegrating from within. I believe we can avoid both a clash of civilizations and Western decline if there is broad understanding that life consists of the circular interplay between order and disorder which, as we shall presently see, characterizes all systems, while humans have gradually become square pegs in that round hole.

Some contemporary thinkers who correctly see the earth as a geological and biological entity of which humans are a part, would have us abandon progress. But it's absurd to think that we could turn our backs on the last ten thousand years of human history. Instead, we need to realize that for most of that time, sharing was unquestioned. It was only when men settled down and began to grow food that the possession of things became paramount. Now that we can produce anything we want or need, we must learn to share again, in a world infinitely more complex than that of hunter-gatherers. The electronic tools that made the Meadows' research possible dominate our lives, but it is the new physics that can help us understand the relationship between Otherness, Being and Having within the Whole of which humans are a part.

"Having" is a familiar notion. "Otherness" refers to the way we perceive of and relate to others. "Being" is a simpler concept than Heidegger's 'Dasein', 'being there' or 'being with the world', that led to existentialism, and was also thought to have been inspired by Oriental philosophy. In this work, 'Being' is based on the confirmation by modern science of the Oriental notion of the-Whole-that-is, the '*tat*' of '*tat tvam asi*' which implies that Being is the only absolute, and hence that it alone should be regarded as sacred.

Ten thousand years ago, the shift from hunter-gathering to agriculture introduced linearity to a world that had been dominated by circular - often magical - thinking. But over the last few centuries, linear thinking's goal of liberating man from endless toil has been perverted, as progress, or modernity, became identified with Having. As Karen Armstrong stresses in *The Battle for God*, for many peoples, modernity is fearful. Muslim and other fundamentalists take advantage of that fear to impose a doctrine that severely limits individual freedom in favor of the group. But fundamentalism exists in every religion, and many non-believing Westerners lament the over-emphasis on individualism that has led to drugs, crime, unemployment and broken families - in a word the lack of community that Islamists seek to remedy.

This work will show that for modernity to be associated with the Good, we need to replace a 3,000 year pursuit of religious Truth with awareness of Being as the only sacred absolute. Once we realize that morality is not dictated by God, but flows from that recognition, we can restore it to the life of a secular polis, with which it must have a relationship.

Although we know that humans evolved from the same elements that gave rise to our planet, that knowledge has been divorced from our everyday lives, and more grievously, from the way we make decisions. Instead of regarding the past as a footnote to our own existence, we need to acknowledge the incredibly long line that stretches from Neanderthal to us. For billions of years, the earth sustained itself by interacting with the biosphere without human intervention. Then, for hundreds of thousands of years, humans lived in a totally different way, not only from the way we live today, but from contemporary 'primitive' groups. Accustomed to thinking in terms of recorded history, which is in fact very short when compared to that of the planet, we have implicitly divorced ourselves from those early ancestors and their environment, as it evolved into the one that is threatened today.

Humans spread out of Africa around 100,000 years ago, but modern man did not arise until 35,000 years ago, and village life only began around 11,000 B.C.. The earliest humans survived under the same conditions as the plants and animals, subject only to the whims of nature. As humanity grew from clan to tribe to chiefdoms, it traded hunting-gathering for agriculture and began to act upon the planet as neither animals nor plants can do. The earliest cities have been dated from 3,700 B.C., which means that complex human activity upon the system Earth has been going on for less than six thousand years. The industrial revolution is less than 500 years old, but it now threatens the planet's ability to support humans. (According to the Old Testament, believed to have been written a millennium or so before Christ, it was God who ordered man to conquer the earth. Or perhaps this was the original adolescent revolt against father elements and mother earth - or the first manifestation of intelligence which early Chinese emperors mistrusted....)

In *Guns, Germs and Steel,* Jared Diamond tells us that starting from the earliest political systems, the crucial question for the elite, which emerged thanks to surplus crops, has been how to keep a maximum of the community's wealth for itself without falling victim to the superior numbers of those who toiled to produce it. Organized religion helped justify the system that Diamond calls kleptocracy, and the oldest religion we can trace existed in Egypt three thousand years before our era. Around the 6th or 5th century B.C., new religious ideas arose simultaneously around the world in the geographic belt located roughly between the Equator and the Tropic of Cancer, in which agriculture had first emerged: the Near East, India, China, Meso-America and the Andes.

A thousand years later, the world was still a fairly homogeneous system; but beginning in the 12th or 13th century A.D., the level of development of the white, northern half of the globe surged ahead of the darker, southern portion, for reasons which Diamond traces to prehistoric geographic and climatic features. And three hundred years after that, the industrial revolution led to the birth of political ideology. By the time the advantages of complexity were imported into the New World, some of Diamond's geographic features had become irrelevant, as the twentieth century piled elaborate political, economic and sociological systems onto earth's physical template, resulting in planetary crisis.

Neither religions nor political systems have been able to overcome the inequality generated by kleptocracy, culminating in a global system that desecrates the human habitat. It is my hope that ancient wisdoms can help us understand the scientific nature of change, so that we may be able to transform struggle into navigation, and politics, instead of trying to dominate the earth and events, can work with the former to steer the latter.

Ideology hides the fact that any system that is out of balance has problems. For most of the twentieth century, the 'haves' weighed more; but with the liberation movements that began in the southern hemisphere after the Second World War, the scale began to tip the other way. Convinced of their enduring superiority, Northern decision-makers failed to realize that they were living in a new era: For the first time in history, a single culture had reached to the four corners of the earth, while the wealth that enabled it did not. And knowledge, formerly a leisurely pursuit for the few that transformed gardens into factories, had become a weapon for the many.

If we compare the world of the twenty-first century to the relatively simple world of a hundred years ago, (viewed, with hindsight, as idyllic), we notice that although it has been greatly transformed, it fits on an iPhone. The mechanic in Brisbane can locate Bagram, and the Blue People of the Sahara compose rap music. Since September 11th, the United States has waged an endless war on terrorism, as progressives cry in the wilderness that problems cannot be solved through violence. Both groups fail to see that the planet consists of interrelated systems of which humans are a part.

However tragic when seen out of context, the horror of September 11th causes us to give it greater significance than were it seen as part of a process, a marker in a worldwide struggle for development. Legitimately, the Third World wants to become 'advanced', while its 'backward' state suits the North's appetite for resources. The antagonism generated by this situation has been simmering for decades, as the largely Christian Caucasian peoples that constitute 20% of humanity continued to consume 70% of the world's resources, pillaged from the south. Confident in their technical ability to outweigh the populations of Asia, Africa, South America and the Indian subcontinent should they decide that globalization shall not pass, Caucasians still fail to realize that they are no longer simply *a* minority among the world's inhabitants, but could be seen as an *absolute minority*.

Having vanquished the Fascists and the Communists, the West thought it had earned the right to a radiant future. But while our leaders cling to a belief in the supremacy of the white man, our youth know otherwise: whatever immigrants do, their sheer numbers provoke the rage of impotence. And hatred of the Other is all the more powerful that it reflects the media that inspires it, even as it allows us to witness its violence. That hatred will not be assuaged by calling in the forces of law and order - or tracking down terrorists.

North Americans, Europeans and Australians can no longer take refuge in cities on a hill, protected by technology. Yet few of their leaders realize we must change the way we relate to the world and work toward sustainable development rather than making war. Because the world's inhabitants are not distributed according to the carrying capacity of its political or geographic entities, a certain measure of population redistribution is inevitable. Right and left argue over the extent to which we can allow the poor of the South to move in with us, but that question became moot when colonization ended: conscious of their majority status, the poor no longer have to knock on the door. As South/North migration increases, the challenge for the North is how to live in a house with no doors, accepting to see its population become the color of honey in all its varieties. As for the South, it needs to realize that hatred does not generate solutions. While daunting, these cultural transformations can come about through the realization that movement and change constitute the essence of Being, as well shall presently see.

Part of the problem is that ideology reflects a basic difference between two types of people: forward and backward looking, open and closed, generous and egotistical, conservative and innovative. In every historical period, there have been masses and elites, each composed of enlightened and obtuse elements. In order for a civilization to endure, the enlightened elites must avoid becoming mired in yesterday's battles, or confronting today's problems using yesterday's paradigms. We defeated the Fascists and the Communists with our technology and our economy, but today we need to realize that the challenge is essentially spiritual and cultural. To define it as 'defeating terrorism' is like saying it is to defeat war. Since the killing of Bin Laden it has become painfully clear that focusing on him was naive, because he was merely a catalyst. A more realistic approach would be to modify our behavior until terrorism loses its purpose.

The most difficult challenge will not be religion, but women's place in an evolving world. What can the West do to assuage the anger of Muslim men, who willingly abdicate their internal authority to the Prophet, when they lose their authority over women? In a sexist world, only a man enjoys the status of enemy, only a man can be the enemy of another. Ethnic cleansing is a perverse form of sexism, in which men rape women seen as belonging to an inferior nationality or race, as if to say: "I humiliate you by subjecting you physically, forcing you to bear my child and, in an ultimate negation of your selfhood, to love him against your will." Hope lies in the fact that the Kurdish Peshmerga fighters - like some African guerrilla forces - include battalions of women in lipstick....

September 11th lit a fuse with a very short wire, shattering the West's display windows with the evidence it refuses to see: that of its gradual dilution in a world where people are as important as chips. In earlier times, if events in one part of the world affected other regions, no one was aware of it. Now, thanks to the media, everything that goes on anywhere is seen by almost everyone. And what people the world over see on their cell-phones can convince them that it is morally right to blow up a skyscraper with human ammunition to avenge the killing of other humans.

But is not terrorism an almost logical culmination of the many ways in which people everywhere seem to be courting death? Perhaps humans have always felt the need to flout death through personal violence because in the beginning, nature was so threatening. But now in the North, youth is ready to die for trivia, while the South's upheavals represent a schizophrenic state of neither-being-nor-having, an indirect result of the North's sacrifice of Being to Having. Even our Eros has become a Having instead of a Being, degenerating into a death instinct, expressed as the destruction of possessions, which in reality is a destruction of the Self. And when we condemn the South for killing people with the same nonchalance as Ghengis Khan, we fail to see that it is merely following the example of the North's gangs and militarism.

Increasingly, the congruence of atrocities committed in the four corners of the world highlights the fact that rejection of the Other has become a worldwide phenomenon. The similarities in the tirades of right-wing politicians from very different cultures is striking. But intolerance, and the breakdown of what conservatives call law and order, are also linked to the exponential rise in the world's population, combined with the notion that people must disregard their need for familiarity and accept to live among strangers. Although touted as the epitome of enlightenment, a world organized into states en-globing several peoples has resulted in the increasing use of surveillance and force by governments against their own people. That situation, coupled with the 2008 financial crisis, brought a new awareness that community is more important than consumption.

Other periods have had their craziness, but never to such an extent. We are an auto-referential society that watches itself watch itself go down the drain. Fascinated by catastrophe, we talk to emphasize our inability to act. We think, discuss, debate, divorced from what we're thinking, writing, talking about. Unless a way can be found to reverse the present destructive trend that pervades Western society and encourages movements like Al Qaeda and ISIS, the North/South divide could lead to the disappearance of the North as we know it without resolving the problems of the South.

I'll argue in what follows that the same changes that could help the South become more peaceful, could contribute to a renewal of the North. They include balancing external authority with increased internal authority; a spirituality based on sacredness rather than faith; an economic foundation that requires less consumption and therefore less competition; respect for life, a concomitant acceptance of death, and a new relationship with Nature.

Linear thinking assumes that problems are solved through military alliances. I am suggesting a different type of alliance, whose nature and participants are a function of Otherness in its relationship to spirituality, sovereignty and violence. That alliance flows from an understanding of a few basic scientific notions that can be extrapolated to human affairs.

II
From There to Here

*Without desire we can see
its secret. With desire we can
see its limits.*
Tao te King

Before we tackle these scientific notions, it is worth considering how the relatively predictable North of the early twentieth century evolved into the shambles we experience today. Thanks in part to its colonization of the South, it was a qualitatively better place than it is now.

The changes that brought us from there to here flow from the sacralization of individual freedom. The Second World War not only marked man's ability to destroy the earth; it constituted a sociological watershed, epitomized by the Freudian revolution. By the sixties, Freud's social theories were being challenged, among others, by Herbert Marcuse, a philosopher who fled Nazi Germany to teach in California, and became a contentious exponent of freedom as an absolute.

Freud believed external authority to be an indispensable component of civilization, while Marcuse maintained that it compromised individual freedom. If the references that follow go beyond a few quotations, it's because here as elsewhere in this work, rather than a specific point, it's an outlook that I want to emphasize.

Marcuse, who wrote about politics from a psychological yet highly ideological point of view, is perhaps best known for *One Dimensional Man*, but the work discussed in this chapter is *Eros and Civilization*. In it Marcuse took exception to Freud's contention that constraints imposed by society are the indispensable condition of progress, and that human history is about repression. According to Freud, if men were allowed to pursue the objectives dictated by their basic instincts, these would prove incompatible with "constructive association or reliable protection". When Eros has no boundaries, it is as fatal as its counterpart, Thanatos, the death instinct, both of which constantly clamor for satisfaction. Freud describes repression as the transformation of the pleasure principle into the reality principle, which, by bringing security, protects the pleasure principle. He maintained that happiness must be subordinated to full-time work, the discipline of monogamous reproductive behavior and the law, and that the systematic sacrifice of the libido to socially useful activities is what defines civilization.

Pointing to the growing effectiveness of domination in all the industrial societies, to constraint Marcuse opposed pleasure with a capital P. Concentration camps, genocide and nuclear bombs, he said, were not momentary regressions into barbarianism, but the result of technology and domination. Seeing the ever more efficient destruction of man by man entrenched at the highest levels of civilization, just when material and intellectual achievements seemed to make possible a truly free world, he inspired the sixties motto 'make love not war'. Taking aim at Freud's *Civilization and its Discontents*, he proposed a different analysis of the general disorder it described, not so much from an overwhelming interest in psychoanalytical theory, but as an intellectual committed to social change.

According to Marcuse, psychological categories become political categories when individuals allow society to dictate their satisfactions. He claimed that qualitative social transformation could lead to a nonrepressive society, in which not only work time would be reduced to a minimum, but also that taken up by what he called "active and passive activities imposed by the dominant group". While admitting that contemporary society allowed for non-repressive activities, Marcuse claimed that this semblance of freedom soon became a vehicle of stabilization and conformism, leaving intact, and even sustaining, a pervasive type of oppression. In this he anticipated the communication society that today maintains humans in a servitude that is not always physical, but is definitely spiritual. Whatever one may think of Marcuse's call for total freedom, when reading this statement it's difficult not to admire its prescience: few individual activities escape mediation by the techno-commercial establishment.

Less impressive, however, was Marcuse's conviction that if the pleasure principle were transformed into action, it would alter reality, increasing desires while providing individuals with the means to satisfy them. He affirmed that neither our desires nor their ability to alter reality any longer belonged to us, but were organized by a society that modified our original instinctive needs. While I agree with Marcuse's diagnosis, I disagree with his conviction that absolute freedom is the answer. Children whose mothers followed Dr. Spock's methods prolonged demand feeding ad infinitum, never growing up. Although Marcuse's moral imperative of freedom, clothed in the raiments of pleasure, was only picked up by a handful of students and hippies in California, as youth increasingly pursued the happiness promised by Madison Avenue, fewer and fewer turned out to vote, allowing government and industry to strengthen their domination of society.

Which of these two thinkers was right? Although their opinions clashed, I believe both were wrong. Marcuse was a man of the left, like Spartacus, while Freud considered himself a man of the right, like Moses. Yet Marcuse and Freud, like Moses and Spartacus, were linear thinkers. And they led us into a wall.

Marcuse accused capitalist society of using freedom to continue the repression necessary to its ends. Realizing that youth were constantly introjecting- or owning - their masters' orders, accepting the repression that inevitably followed rebellion, in typically linear fashion he enjoined them to be 'really free'. Calling on them to refuse all constraints, he overlooked the fact that constraints are part of nature. Crucially, he failed to see that unlimited freedom cannot be found in action but is a state of being. Although he correctly foresaw that as work time lessened, leisure would increase, with free time rather than labor time determining how men lived, his expectation that increased leisure would allow for the free play of each individual's faculties has not been borne out.

Marcuse believed that a modification of the relationship between the two areas of human reality, pleasure and work, would change the relationship between instinct and reason, between what is desirable and what is reasonable. He thought that as sexuality was transformed into Eros, life instincts would develop their own order, and reason would become so sensitive that it would "use organized necessity to protect and enrich life instincts. The roots of the esthetic experience would reemerge, not only in the arts, but in the fight for survival, creating a new rationality". But pleasure cannot be opposed to reality because reality consists of pleasure and pain. Work and play, Yin and Yang, instinct and reason, are not antithetical, which is why they cannot be associated with the notion of progress or lack thereof. To date, "liberated" esthetic experience has been largely confined to reality TV.

The notion of progress is implicit in the belief Marcuse shared with philosophical anarchists, that men will eventually administer things rather than other men, and that coordinated measures would bring about an 'adult' civilization. Like anarchists, Marcuse foresaw a 'recognized and recognizable authority based on knowledge and necessity', such as traffic cops and pilots. However, he emphasized the conflict between individual and group freedom, rather than the notion of individual responsibility espoused by anarchists. Individual freedom is not only a private affair, he said, but it is nothing if it is not also a private affair. He believed that "from the moment private life had no need to be separated and even opposed to public life, individual and group freedom could be reconciled through a general will, via institutions whose purpose is the satisfaction of individual needs". But this begs the question, for both individual and group freedom are limited, and as we shall see in what follows, both have a relationship to the science-based moral imperative of protecting Being, or the Whole, of which humans are a part.

Marcuse affirmed that instinct was beyond good and evil and that Eros had its own self control, contained in the notion that satisfaction requires postponements. When limits and restrictions were not imposed by the outside world, they would be accepted for their libidinal value. When they were required by the general will, they would neither be incomprehensible nor inhuman, anymore than their reason for being would be authoritarian. He affirmed that even Freud defended this position when he wrote that "to blossom, the libido requires obstacles". Marcuse claimed that when no longer used to maintain men (and women!) in alienating activities, barriers against absolute satisfaction would become elements of human freedom. We would truly exist as individuals, each creating his/her own life, with different needs and choices. The primacy of the pleasure principle would provoke conflicts over satisfaction, but these would also have libidinal value because they would be permeated by the rationality of satisfaction. Thumbing his nose at Hegel, who at least distinguished between reason and desire, he claimed that 'sensitive rationality' would have its own moral laws.

Marcuse admitted that the question remains: "How can civilization produce freedom freely, when slavery has become an integral part of our mentality?" And if it cannot, who has the right to determine the objective criteria? Unfortunately, he was content to hope that society would find the right way through trial and error, but thus far instinct has not refused instant satisfaction, eroticizing non-libidinous relations and transforming biological tension and release into 'liberated happiness'.

Though he was a social scientist, Marcuse used the linear 'if.......then' type of reasoning found in mathematics. Starting from the premise that there exist such things as absolute freedom, objective criteria or Truth, to repression, however subtle, he opposed total freedom, in a tit for tat ideology. He wished for an end to repression because he believed that would allow us to fully realize our potential for all that is good in life. But his wish was based on the erroneous assumption that personal fulfillment can be obtained from outside the Self: absolute freedom has repressed the Marcuse generation in ways he never imagined, enslaving many to drugs and less directly damaging Things.

The dramatic increase in violence the world has witnessed is partly a result of the supremacy of the very pleasure principle from which Marcuse expected a softening influence. Not because there is anything inherently wrong with pleasure, but because it should not be divorced from the notion of responsibility. When limits and restrictions are no longer imposed by the outside world, far from becoming elements of human freedom, they are negated and ultimately abolished. The path late twentieth century youth followed in refusing to 'auto-repress' itself gradually led to a near breakdown of society, with conflict as the dominant *modus operandi*.

I will make the case that we can only limit the power of external authority by reconquering individual internal authority, or inner freedom. The consequences that followed upon the implementation of Marcuse's theories show that life is circular, with each action setting off a series of interactions and retroactions that create a host of unforeseen consequences. Our sexual drives may no longer be repressed, but our need for love has been bent out of recognition. And security, which Freud claimed could only be maintained through certain constraints, has evaporated.

The American Indians believe that the circle encompasses the universe, yet is reassuring; everything tries to be round, and as long as the circle is unbroken, the people flourish. They strive to maintain contact between their young and nature, convinced that when man strays from nature his heart becomes hard, lack of respect for living things leading to a lack of respect for humans. The individual is at once responsible for and linked to nature, and each of us must meet the sun and the Great Silence alone in the morning.

The linear illusion of unlimited freedom leads individuals to go nature many better in order to live a more decent life than their neighbor. This is a closed circle that becomes ever smaller the more it is centered on man, driving him to extinction. By giving the individual an ever greater place, society weakens the circle until there is nothing left to reassure him. We see this when a small child is made the center of attention. Even as she manipulates the adults focusing on her every whim, their desire to respect her will drains her of that will. A desperate anxiety creeps into her eyes, which seems to be saying: "Where is my Self?"

You don't have to be a religious fundamentalist to notice that Muslim children who are brought up in a firm yet loving environment appear to have a greater sense of security than our Western children brought up with too much freedom and too little warmth by overstressed parents. Today, Islam is the most forceful reaction against the cultural revolution of which Marcuse was the prophet. The fact that it too is based on linear premises, demanding that society be based on Shari'a law, does not make Islam's rejection of the society Marcuse helped inspire any less valid.

This last half century has destroyed not only enormous areas of the material world that humans built up over the centuries, but also crucial parts of our inner world that evolved over millennia. The idea of freedom is so central to our culture that it is difficult for us to believe that more of it is not necessarily better. We fear the violence of fundamentalists, and see no way out of the Us-Them situation created by their refusal to envy our loss.

We can now turn to science to show that there is no such thing as absolute freedom, not even for the most powerful nation the world has ever known.

III
Order/Disorder

*Neither words nor deeds can harm your
mind. Once it has become a sphere,
perfectly round, it remains that way.*
Marcus Aurelius

Since the Second World War, Washington's policies have been those of a powerful nation confronting
a series of enemies of its own deliberate creation, in
order to feed an economic system based on consumption. Islamic extremism having replaced Communism
as the latest threat, even sophisticated analysts over-
look a crucial detail: 'The West' owes its forward-
looking lifestyle to the same linear thinking from
which Communism derives its aspirations and Islam
its backward-looking crusade. Judaism, Christianity
and Islam all involve a God who stands above and
apart from a world in which good and evil confront
each other, and that mindset infuses their corresponding political systems. Very differently, the Oriental
religions, Buddhism, Taoism and Hinduism are circular: life and death are part of a process of eternal renewal, and the only question is how to live in the here
and now.

Beginning in the nineties, America witnessed an
extensive 'God vs. the Cosmos' debate, with a pleth-
ora of books by atheists such as Richard Dawkins and
Christopher Hitchens. Although they base their posi-

tion on science, most atheist writers ignore the con-
nection between modern science and non-deistic spirituality that has been recognized by science writers like
the popular Gary Zukav and scientists like Fritjof Capra and others who will also be introduced here.

The 1960s counter-culture tried, but failed, to
move America from religion to spirituality, partly because the public could not see beyond its external
manifestations: drugs and dropping out. Interestingly,
The Limits to Growth made its appearance just as the
counter-culture was waning, yet thirty years later, it is
still not widely applied to political analysis. Perhaps
that is because few people who work with scientific
concepts are interested in politics, while political analysts tend to be scientifically challenged. When I began my enquiry into attitudes toward death and religion, after spending decades observing various political
regimes and learning about systems theory, it was the
work of Alan Watts, the counter-culture's spiritual
guru who reigned in tandem with Marcuse, its political theoretician, that first drew my attention to the
similarities between modern science and ancient wisdoms. Those revelations were for me nothing short of
an epiphany, because they put an irrefutable foundation under a life-long commitment to reason, while
providing a rhapsodic substitute for religious dogma
and rituals. Their relevance to politics was the cherry
on the cake.

Watts, an Anglican clergyman, had noticed in the
fifties that cybernetics was the modern version of oriental philosophy. He moved to California and introduced his ideas to college youth. Although he rejected
the possibility of a meeting between science and relig-

ion, since his death in 1973 the similarities between cybernetics and the religions without God have received so much attention that perhaps he would not do so now.

Always, there have been civilizations in which thinking was more linear, where each entity had an opposite, each cause an effect, each action its response; and others in which the accent was on the circular interdependence of opposites rather than differences. The American Indians, who crossed the Bering Straits from Asia in prehistoric times, still practice circular thinking on the reservations to which they have been relegated. In this they resemble Hindus, Buddhists, Taoists, animists - and opponents of globalization.

Modern man sees himself in a linear relationship with a world that is outside himself, to be dominated by states entertaining linear relations with each other. But twentieth century science established that the world is not separate from man, he and it are one, their various elements in constant, recursive interaction. *The Limits to Growth* was followed by many other works showing that linear concepts and straight line projections do not reflect reality. Reality is a complex intermingling of processes that must be considered together with the repercussions of each on all the others if we are to have some control over our lives. Repercussions create new situations that must be taken into account when initiating further actions, or simply trying to deal with those under way. Unforeseeable interactions between repercussions set off unpredictable consequences, while our ability to control this process diminishes in inverse proportion to its accel-

pharmaceuticals..

eration. The graph below shows how feedback loops, the basis of cybernetics and theoretical models, counter-balance each other.

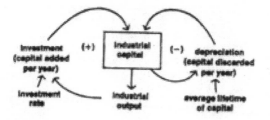

The subject is industrial output, where capital is assumed to be the limiting factor in production, and some part of profits are reinvested to increase capital stock. There are two feedback loops, one positive, the other negative. While more capital creates more output in a positive feedback loop, the depreciation of capital stock diminishes it in a negative one.

Circular, recursive, co-operative relations are more enhancing than those that result from linear, tit for tat behavior. Involving interactions between all the phenomena involved in, or resulting from, human activity, circular relations diminish hierarchies; integrating repercussions at all levels. Blurring the notions of strength/weakness, subject/object, victors/vanquished, they lead to a softening of conflict-ridden situations; the identity for which citizens are ready to die moves a bit further away on the space continuum, while at closer proximity, those of neighborhood, town and region flourish. The increasingly global nature of economics may make it easier to accept circular concepts than it was thirty years ago, in particular if they make sense in practical terms. Although the Meadows' did not spell out the ecological threat caused by global warming, we are now over-shooting survival thresholds, or what they called 'ultimately sustainable levels'.

But how does knowing this help in our war against fundamentalist terrorism? Twenty years ago, James Lovelock published a wonderful book called *Planetary Medicine* to illustrate what he called the Gaia theory. The earth and the biosphere are seen as an organism, and stunning illustrations show the natural phenomena that create and maintain life on earth. Besides being fascinating, Gaia helps us understand why socio-political problems enable terrorism. The human needs that Al Qaeda and its off-shoots exploit represent what we could call deep wounds on the face of the planet earth. Imagine a human organism whose head and chest, benefiting from certain natural conditions, have developed splendidly, while the rest of the body is mired in a series of debilitating diseases. Wouldn't the arms and legs do everything they could to deprive the healthy part of the body of sustenance in order to heal themselves?

Human survival today is linked to the health of the planet, which includes not only levels of CO_2 in the atmosphere, or the acidification of the oceans, but also, the well-being of its inhabitants. Among others, a look at the history of the Muslim world shows that it has deep wounds, while the rest of the world's need for oil stands in the way of their healing. And yet, political discourse fails to recognize that terrorist attacks could be met with a dialogue about what is ailing the planetary body. Instant and exhaustive news calls for bandaids. Playing to our emotions, it neglects the big picture and the long view of events which is where the answers lie.

The challenge for the North today is to navigate a rapidly changing world with the lowest cost in blood and treasure. It requires us to replace tit for tat policies with a systemic approach that takes into account the multifarious geographic, climatic and political characteristics of the planet that together form a system. When we refer to political systems, we usually mean an arrangement or a practice corresponding to words such as 'democracy', 'monarchy', 'communism'. These labels hide the fact that a political system is also a system in the scientific sense: a group of related elements in which the modification of one element modifies the whole.

Before moving any further toward an understanding of systems, it will be useful to take a short detour to Darwin's theory of evolution. At the time of this biological discovery, physics had shown that left to itself, a system eventually runs down, yet this new theory seemed to imply that systems could go on forever! Physicists were in an uproar over this seeming contradiction until the Russian Ilya Prigogyne realized that mechanical systems are described by linear equations, while the behavior of living systems could only be described by non-linear equations.

You don't have to know anything about equations to accept the fact that living and non-living entities are translated mathematically using different types of signs. What Prigogyne was saying is that yes, life is based on natural selection, as Darwin affirmed, but because living systems are open to their environment, from which, via feedback, they receive matter and energy and into which they reject waste, they can, in theory, go on forever. Very differently, non-living, or mechanical systems inevitably run down because they are separated from, or closed to their environment and its sources of energy.

Feedback has been expressed since ancient Chinese times as the opposites Yin/Yang growing out of each other. The Chinese knew instinctively that change occurs as a result of action by each element in the dyad on the other, as many scientists today recognize, while people focusing on spirituality see that Yin/Yang also stands for oneness, or Unicity. Consider the following lines from the Taoist canon, the *Tao te Ching*:

> The Tao is like a well: used but never emptied.
> It is like the eternal void filled with infinite possibilities.
> The heavy is the root of all light.
> The unmoved is the source of all movement.

At this crucial point, as a numerically challenged writer I'm counting on my enthusiasm for the fact that the second law of thermodynamics resembles ancient wisdom to dissuade similarly challenged readers from turning away. They will be rewarded with a clarification of right and left's seeming contradictory positions on human life which, as a bonus, reveals a narrow opening in the wall that opposes Islamic and Western world-views. I apologize in advance to the scientific community for the liberties I may be taking with exactitude. Here as in the rest of this book, it is the gist rather than the detail that is relevant.

Briefly, energy inputs into a system organize molecules to do work, creating what physicists counter-intuitively call 'order'. Lack of energy eventually results in a state of 'equilibrium' or 'entropy', which physicists call 'disorder'. Ideally, as the Taoists intuited, the flow of energy through a system keeps it 'just far enough from equilibrium' to avoid entropy - or death. But any number of factors can cause that flow to increase, creating runaway instability. A certain amount of instability is necessary for things to happen, but too much instability takes the system so far from equilibrium that it eventually reaches a threshold known as a bifurcation point, from which it 'dissipates' into a new state (hence the name 'dissipative system' given by Prigogyne to what are also known as open systems).

Born from chaos, order is not static but dynamic, while counter-intuitively, it is disorder that is static. The ever-changing relationship between the two is a delicate balancing that a rush of energy can push 'too far from equilibrium' to endure. When that happens, the system dissipates, either creating new order, - or life - or breaking down. It is impossible to predict which will happen; as with forecasting in general, that depends on previous history.

The components of political 'systems' include human, geographic, historical and cultural elements. I refer to them as being 'closed', because the many are largely kept outside deliberations by the few. Dictatorship, which seeks to maintain a status quo, or, in scientific terms, 'equilibrium', inevitably leads to the political system's death when revolution opens it to the many that have been kept outside it, constituting its 'environment'. (We shall have more to say about political systems in what follows. Books that help understand systems theory, the best of which are Fritjof Capra's *The Web of Life,* and his most recent and exhaustive *The Systems View of Life,* are listed in the bibliography.)

But physics is not the only science that contributes to the understanding of political systems. Neurobiology's contribution is less well-known, but I find it even more exciting. In the 1970's, Chilean scientists Humberto Maturana and Francisco Varela realized that life does not consist of 'things', but of processes. What feedback does is enable an organism (which is a system) to assimilate information, and this processing of information, which biologists call 'cognition', is what creates new life!

Varela and Maturana called this process 'self-making' and crafted a Greek-inspired term, autopoiesis, to express it. Fritjof Capra elegantly defines autopoiesis as "a network pattern in which the function of each component is to participate in the production or trans-formation of other components via the circular organization of information through multiple feedback loops which constantly correct imbalances. In this process, spontaneous patterns emerge to create self-organization and self- making."

You may have to read this definition several times, but doing so will reveal a totally new picture of life. For me, the fact that Being emerges from non-Being in an on-going process of self-creation implies, first of all, that Being is the only absolute, and therefore it, rather than Truth, or God, is sacred. Knowing that every living thing and every process is not only characterized by a counter-balancing of order and disorder, but also by constant self-making eliminates the monopoly of ideology, and twenty-first century democracy in favor of men and women playing direct roles in the ordering of their affairs.

All species are involved in self-making, but only humans have replaced this natural process with doing. Doing involves interactions between a multitude of living organisms, human, plant and mineral - all open systems - and the mechanical, or closed systems we create. Is it any wonder that alone among animals, humans 'have problems'? The constant interplay of order/disorder multiplies bifurcations, making outcomes difficult to predict and control. And the resulting high levels of human stress are rarely relieved by the actions of closed socio-political systems.

When we observe the demonstrations of occupied Palestinians, Greek workers or American students, it's clear that the planet's various body parts are so far from equilibrium that bifurcations are inevitable. And here's the kicker: in physics, the arrow of time is irreversible, meaning that once popular discontent reaches a certain level, it will more likely lead to revolution than revert to a former peaceful situation (known as putting the genie back in the bottle). Most revolutions can be seen as catalysts that turn a state of extreme order into one of extreme disorder, while most disintegrations of empire result from the entropy to which extreme order leads

It's not because men are inherently evil that there are more problems than pleasures in life, but because the order/disorder dyad implies that any durable domination of immobility, or equilibrium, over instability, signifies death. According to Stephen Hawking and other scientists, the universe contains slightly more matter than antimatter; it also appears that negative and positive energy cancel each other out, and that gravity can under some circumstances act as a repulsive force. Mass and energy, waves and particles, energy and entropy, O and 1, all exhibit the oneness-in-change that characterizes the order/disorder dyad, which the Chinese call Yin/Yang.

Scientists describe these facts using equations, but the rest of us can simply accept them, as do the Chinese, because they imply certain things for the way we live our lives. (Gary Zukav's amusing presentation in the seventies bestseller *The Dancing Wu Li Masters,* makes them highly accessible.) Order/disorder is the way life is. And because instability is indispensable for any system to evolve, it invariably maintains a slight upper hand. That's why life seems so difficult, why, in a word things 'always happen to us', why the other shoe eventually drops, why politics is so important - and why it so often fails to solve our problems.

We wonder whether man can survive in space and under what conditions. But what does it mean when human life breaks with the self-making that occurs in consonance with other species and the natural environment, to pursue a different type of self-making for the purpose of adapting to a mechanical environment it has created?

In just one century, the psychological structures humans had known throughout their evolution from ape to hominid, composed of kinship groups and families, have been almost totally destroyed. We have reached a point where unforeseen consequences resulting from the feedback between technology, history, geography and sociology could render our planet incompatible with human life. Yet as products of a linear culture, we insist on confronting life's personal and societal challenges in a dualistic, tit for tat mode. Blind to the circular reality of life, we not only fight the Other, we try in vain to adapt to the closed systems we have created by confronting machines, germs, and toxins, to name but a few.

Circular thinking helps us understand that human societies are characterized by the same counter-balancing of order and disorder as life itself. Negotiations of every sort, whether involving labor and management, globalization or a divorce, require the delicate counter-balancing of opposing demands that satisfies both parties and is known as compromise. By definition, liberal democracy cannot meet this requirement, because, like its predecessors, it is a closed system that runs on the energy of a small group of insiders. Diamond's kleptocrats, or oligarchs, maintain a status quo 'just far enough from equilibrium' until outsiders force enough energy into the system to take it to a bifurcation that opens it, taking its energy from them and rejecting previous decisions as waste.

The fact that technology now makes it possible for a single human being to create global disruptions - or dissipations - does not negate the value of systems thinking. Right and wrong are linear, dualistic categories, while cultures - and politics - are systemic processes. Bin Laden's affirmation that Western cultural behaviors are wrong, and our affirmation that they are right, both deny that. While even Atheists agree that loss of morality plays a role in our disarray, and most Muslims are horrified by terrorism, immersed in linear cultures that view the world in black and white, neither can for the moment bifurcate to a higher level of civilization.

For that to happen, global society would have to move from linear, dualistic thinking to circular thinking, and from religion, that denies the Other in favor of Having, to the notion of Unicity - or Oneness - that enhances Being. 'Being' means living in awareness of belonging to the Whole. 'Having' means living to acquire ever more of the Whole. Being is an open system that creates life. Having is a closed system, a finality in itself, in whose name humans have gradually renounced cognition, unloading the task of processing information to machines, turning our selves into frozen receptacles instead of beings constantly involved in self-making.

By foraging for food, organizing a hunt, making our own dwellings and clothes, we evolved from apes to hominids to humans. But when we settled down, built cities, and eventually went to the moon, we cut ourselves off from the earth, the system, or Whole, of which we are a part. Unicity reconnects us to the Whole by making sacredness the only absolute, and seeing Others and their needs as an indissoluble part of Being.

Many factors led to the present situation, but since the industrial revolution, and especially since Hiroshima, these factors have multiplied exponentially, giving rise to an ever greater number of people who do not want the complete package the so-called indispensable nation has created. Oblivious to the fact that Yin and Yang, the intuitive and the rational, are essential to life, the world thrashes hopelessly about in a sea of order/disorder, failing to recognize that our striving for the former is inseparable from the latter. Two decades into e-commerce and the imposition of globalization, no scientific evidence allows us to assume that the next bifurcation will lead to a higher level of civilization, in which earth remains hospitable to humans.

Thirty years after the death of Alan Watts and the publication of *The Limits to Growth*, the alliance between man and nature implicit in their messages is clearly the only solid foundation for dealing with the problématique, making it not only desirable but imperative. The fact that we are not separate from nature, but part of it, suggests that this is no Utopia - an intellectual construct - but a systemic evolution that can be achieved by the same processes that brought humans into being. If we couple the products of our technology with the autopoietic processing of information that will grow us psychologically, creating circular interactions with Others instead of seeking to acquire more Things, we should be able to move away from the brink of disaster toward a far-from-equilibrium state that could go on indefinitely.

IV
Self-Making

The transition between order and chaos
appears to be the regime that optimizes
average fitness for the whole system.
Stuart Kauffman

Noting how difficult it is for modern societies to achieve this transformation, in his elegant *At Home in the Universe*, the biologist Stuart Kauffman points out that:

> The universe is not in equilibrium. Instead of the featureless homogeneity of a vessel of gas molecules, there are differences, potentials, that drive the formation of complexity. Networks in the regime near the edge of chaos, a compromise between order and surprise, appear best able to coordinate complex activities and best able to evolve as well. Yet each is eventually driven to extinction, despite its own best efforts, by the collective behavior of the system as a whole. Life is a globally near-equilibrium structure destined to end.

Kauffman describes three possible states that societies can be in: equilibrium, near equilibrium - both closed systems - or a far-from-equilibrium, open state that takes energy from its environment and evolves toward a new dynamic regime. Paraphrasing Kauffman's remarks, when an open system arrives at the 'edge of chaos', the point of instability that precedes dissipation, it may bifurcate to become an ordered regime (oligarchy), where there is no compromise, or a chaotic regime (representative democracy), where compromises are often poor. However, when participatory democracy - or counterbalancing - allows a system to maintain a stable state just far enough from equilibrium, relatively good compromises can be achieved.

A stable state is not immobile, and one of the reasons why even at its best, democracy doesn't solve all our problems, is that we cannot accept the idea of life being sustained at the edge of chaos, to be eventually followed by dissipation. Oblivious to the fact that there is no definitive, final state, in our determination to achieve 'it', we overrun everything in our path, opting out of the processes followed by other life forms.

As Kauffman reminds us, a cell adapts to its environment; it's not the other way around. Originally, human society, like the rest of nature, was an open system in constant interaction with its environment. It was only after billions of years of self-making that, in the historical period, man began to remake his environment. He continued to take in ordered structures (food) as resources for his metabolism; but instead of allowing waste - a dissipative structure that is close to entropy - to be recycled into the environment where it can recreate food/energy, he transforms some of it into Things and allows the rest to accumulate.

Today's environmental crisis results from a lack of open system exchange: neither the waste generated by machines nor that resulting from the creation of Things can be recycled into nature. And as we try to adapt to the closed environment we have created, we subject ourselves to increasingly elaborate systems of external authority. Suffice it to evoke the fundamental difference between a tribal circle and an elected government to realize how decisively we have lost our individual internal authority and hence, a voice in the decision-making process.

References to citizens being actors of their lives invariably have a hollow ring because they do not reflect the primacy of internal authority. Too busy acquiring things instead of engaging in psychological self-making, we increasingly defer to external authority. At this point in our evolution, we need to recover our internal authority and grow our ability to respect that of others. I will argue here that conscious self-making, or autopoiesis, enhances internal authority, which in turn enables us to resist the dictates of external authority and renew our symbiotic relationship to the environment: to be at once of the Whole and actors of the Whole.

To be sure, resistance to external authority eventually led to democracy, which theoretically constitutes a balancing between two extremes - or what Prigogyne calls order floating in a sea of disorder. In reality, however, masquerading as a Yin/Yang system (now I win now you win) in representative, or liberal democracy it is external authority in the form of money that determines outcomes. 'Democracy' promotes external authority as the opposite of anarchy, and often as its only alternative, when in fact, the opposite of anarchy is totalitarianism.

Only participatory democracy based on each citizens' individual internal authority allows for a flexible consensus that respects the ever-changing natural environment and the needs of all within it. Reliance on external authority to administer the hierarchical controls inherent in all systems is ineffective because these are too rigid to constitute effective counterbalancing. According to the evolutionist Ervin Laszlo, "hierarchical controls arise from internal constraints that force lower-level units into a pattern of collective behavior that is independent of the details of their individual behavior." In a wonderful science-based description of bureaucracy, Laszlo tells us that this occurs via "the selective disregard, on the higher, controlling level, of the detailed dynamics of the lower-level units".

Bureaucracies, and all other forms of higher-level systems, can be contrasted to the higher level of consciousness that characterizes internal authority. And totalitarianism can be seen as a system of control that practices extreme neglect on the lower levels of society until disorder and entropy - i.e., the failure of cognition and internal authority - lead to the system's death through bifurcation.

The Communautarian theorist Amitai Etzioni describes the ideal state of society as symbiosis, expressed as $+X$ and $+Y$. He posits that when X increases substantially more than Y, symbiosis is broken, or inverted, turning to antagonism. In systemic terms, we could say that an increase of X or Y corresponds to a rupture in the far-from-equilibrium stable state in which participatory democracy flourishes. Antagonism is more complex than symbiosis and increases the likelihood that the bifurcation that eventually follows a steady state will lead to a break-down - commonly referred to as anarchy. For the opposite and equally inevitable reason, anarchy will be followed by totalitarianism. Because we are dealing with a living system, eventually, cognition acts on the increasing entropy created by totalitarianism, and the system opens again. This happened in Eastern Europe in 1989. However since totalitarianism is a non-symbiotic system, it can take cognition a while to bring change. Twenty-five years after the collapse of the Soviet Union, Russian civil society is only now coming into its own through a process of autopoiesis fostered by Vladimir Putin.

Given all these caveats, what should be the job of politics? Clearly, it should not be about substituting one group of rulers for another, because rulers, whoever they are, whatever their origins, will always take advantage of their position, going as far as their subjects allow.

The job of politics should be seen as the never-ending process of managing the oscillations between instability and entropy, or order/disorder.

At present, believing that the future can be better than the present, the left tries to determine bifurcations, playing sorcerer's apprentice. The right, believing that the present, or even the past, is preferable to any future, bets on reversibility, denying the fact that the arrow of time is irreversible. Both deny life's essence, which is movement, change and transformation.

Marxism and dialectical materialism are the most elaborately codified systems for influencing events, replacing order/disorder with thesis and anti-thesis, but wrongly concluding that the resulting synthesis can be definitive. As for liberalism, instead of influencing the way the tension between order and disorder plays out, it too often reflects society's desire to out-wit reality, running away from the task of delicate adjustment that constitutes symbiosis (X/Y, or Yin/Yang), rushing into, instead of proceeding toward, the order that results from bifurcation and change, or languishing in the disorder that leads to entropy and immobility. Both right and left ignore the fact that counter-balancing, a dynamic state in the on-going flux between order and disorder, between entropy which leads to death, and the magic moment of bifurcation that can lead to satisfaction or catastrophe, is 'the way things are'.

The French philosopher Françoís Jullien, who coined that notion, likens counter-balancing to the middle ground, or wisdom, of Taoism or Confucianism. Here, I try to apply pragmatically the intuition that counter-balancing is the ongoing reconciliation of seeming opposites that is indispensable to life.

When lack of information-processing causes a system to tend toward immobility, the extremes of left and right - or catalysts such as Bin Laden or Al-Baghdadi - kickstart counter-balancing again, leading eventually to new bifurcations. Seeing the terrorist campaign in its systemic role is neither a Pollyanna attitude nor cynicism, but recognition that we are part of a system in which order and disorder are in constant interplay.

Taking into account the new sciences, it becomes clear that finding guidelines for the next millennium will not depend on whether we look at things from right or left, but on whether our political actors can recognize 'the way things are'. The problems of under-development in the South and unemployment in the North cut across what were once solid lines. Fundamentalism affects not only Muslims, but also Christians and Jews, Liberals and Conservatives, young and old, men and women, and it is saying things about modern society that need urgently to be recognized.

If Islam stands out as the greatest deliberate threat, it's because some Muslims fall into step behind leaders who call for a linear, crime/retribution response to the North's linear crime and drug ridden civilization. Like Judaism and Christianity, Islam is based on the linear concept of one God (Us-Him). Like Fascism and Communism, it rallies masses around an Us-Them situation (believers and infidels). But that very same linear thinking has led the West to believe that progress is a straight line that never ends, instead of one that will eventually reach a bifurcation point that could end in planetary disaster.

The disappearance of the Evil Empire left Americans unprepared to meet new challenges. We are told that we're fighting an Evil Ideology, yet it is incontrovertible that the South cannot develop without sharing in the North's riches. When development in the South leads to loss of jobs in the North rather than markets for its goods, linear thinking sees a problem 'out there' to which we must do things for 'it' to go away, rather than a series of interrelated problems of which we are a part. There is no material reason why populations and resources should not be more harmoniously balanced, if they are viewed as part of a Whole. The North has to lose jobs in order for the South to gain jobs, but northern workers need not be unemployed, because climate change dictates shorter working days, allowing jobs to be shared, as the South steps into our manufacturing shoes.

When we say: "We have seen the enemy and he is us", we're saying that whatever the problem, we are not outside it, nor separate from it, but, part of it. Problems - or chaos - are essential to life, and cannot be solved with tit for tat policies, but only by acting simultaneously on the systemic imbalances that exist at each moment. The realization that we cannot achieve a perfect, immobile state, while painful in superficial ways, such as the requirement that the North renounce some its 'stuff', will allow us to move from the box labeled "absolute minority" - with the consequences this entails - to that labelled "community." Colonization was a linear process in which the ideological flow went from North to South (the conversion of 'savages' into 'good Christians'). Today, that flow goes from South to North: Islam and Buddhism are both making converts, the Non-Aligned Movement has been revitalized - and the BRICS foreshadow a multipolar world.

Humans are the only creatures to use their minds auto-referentially. But the first thing that happened when we said 'I', is that we created the Other. From then on, our cognitive efforts were directed toward acting on discrete processes, environmental or human, rather than adapting to them; toward conscious, goal-directed exploitation of the system instead of continued self-making. The next stage of autopoiesis must reclaim the internal authority that enables small group initiatives, limiting the scope of external authority.

This can happen if we recognize both our own place as part of the Whole - and the Other's. Only thus will we experience the love and compassion for all life that every religion calls for. Only then will Israelis and Palestinians be able to overcome the traumas of the past and resolve those of the present; and both Americans and Arabs to accept that every Golden Age is inevitably succeeded by another, somewhere else.

In the following chapters, I'll explore Otherness as it relates to freedom, fundamentalism, violence, sovereignty and death in a culture based on linear thinking. Then I'll expand on the circular elements that could help us to transform these relationships, and spell out the ecological, spiritual and material dimension of that transformation.

V
Islam and Otherness

*Each Other is other and each Other is
oneself. This truth is not perceptible
from the other, but is understood from
the self. Thus we say, the other comes
from the self, but the self also depends
on the other.*
Tchouang Tseu

The Other is not only the person who speaks a
different language and owes allegiance to a different
nation. He is any person we cannot bring ourselves to
admit is right - especially if he criticizes us. President
George W. Bush claimed that Muslims hate us because
we're 'free', but what Islamic fundamentalists are re-
acting to, is our specific definition of freedom. While
terrifyingly, they consider it legitimate to impose morality by force of arms, we must ask whether a civilization that kills off its young with drugs, or denies them a
livelihood, is morally superior. We declare war on
crime, delinquency and unemployment, yet no politi-
cian could dare suggest that the Muslim, who gives his
allegiance to God instead of a nation, has valid reasons
for rejecting our way of life.

Although the distorted past that ISIS would revive is unacceptable, we shall only be able to convince
its followers to abandon violence if we can overcome
the violence in our own culture. Dialogue with Islamists
can be fruitful if we admit that the behaviors they call

decadent are rejected many thoughtful Westerners. Modern civilization has spread unchecked for decades, but increasingly, Brazilians, Europeans and secular Turks, oppose it because in reality it is uncivilized.

We are told that Muslims are revolting against the humiliations of colonialism and their own decay. But as Karen Armstrong implies in *The Battle for God*, their decay is to a large extent the result of *our* colonialist enterprise, which left them unprepared for the transformations modernity has worked upon human society.

Why is personal behavior so important to Islam? It's because like Judaism, Islam is not about miracles, but about how men should live. When Muhammed decided that his people needed to become as civilized as the Jews and the Christians, he was referring to both individual behavior and a just society. According to Armstrong, God orders the Muslim community - or umma - to achieve a modicum of solidarity among its members by treating each other with 'justice, equity and respect'. Christ may have been the original Marxist, but the Prophet required daily acts of charity.

It is this commitment to solidarity that motivated many twentieth century Muslim leaders to become clients of the Soviet Union. Although most of the world's poor now realize that Communism is not the answer to their problems, the developed world is only just beginning to understand the urgency of helping the majority of the earth's population to catch up to the minority, as the Soviets tried to do. (In Cuba, this was appreciated; in Afghanistan, it was not.) Unscrupulous secular leaders such as Saddam Hussein or Muhamar Quaddafi have been known to shroud aims other than those of God in their Islamic faith, but this is nothing new. In the

Islamic world, the pendulum has constantly swung between reason and faith, and between different interpretations of the Prophet's behavior as the Perfect Man obedient to God's will. Following Mohammad's death, each religious leader thought he had best understood the Prophet's message. Some embraced power to the detriment of solidarity, while others emulated his mystical union with God.

Although the Prophet had considered women as equals, his successors aligned themselves with Judaism and Christianity's belief in their inferiority prolonging it into the twenty-first century. The treatment of women in Muslim societies illustrates something that is true of all religions: founders are almost always worthy of emulation, their successors rarely. Parts of Sharia law, the subordination of women, and war against infidels, all things we find abhorrent in Islam, were not part of the Qu'ran believed to have been dictated by God to Mohammad.

While Judaism embodies reason (there is only one God), and Christianity emphasizes forgiveness (God saves us), perhaps it is because Islam emphasizes God's power that it is so fervent - and fearful. Moses' God gave men rules, and punished any failure to respect them. Jesus' God also gave rules, but forgave transgressions in return for repentance. Mohammad's God could also forgive, but ordered three prayers a day (later raised by zealots to five), to ensure the rules would be respected.

Long-standing opposing concepts of religion and morality in public life are strengthened today by global inequality and the availability of sophisticated means to communicate and destroy. Europe and the United States have for decades received immigrants from the very Muslim countries they attack in the war against terror. Even those who adopt the culture of their new countries resent attacks on their former homelands, where many still have family. Far-right movements in the North exacerbate the tendency to see new arrivals as enemies. failing to realize that South/North immigration will continue until development in the South begins to catch up with that of the North, a systemic reality that no political movement can alter.

For several decades, Samuel Huntington's *Clash of Civilizations* constituted the bellwether for North-South analysis. Only recently has the question of the basic direction in which the North has been moving since the end of the Second World War been raised by American writers such as Chris Hedges and Morris Berman, and a cohort of European post-modernists. These writers denounce the fact that 'Things' have replaced the support human beings have always enjoyed, that of family, community and - I say this as an atheist - religion. And what, if not the importance of Things, can account for the fact that so many children turn to sects and gangs? Under the guise of progress, it identifies Freedom with Having, a satisfaction obtained from outside the Self, rather than with awareness of belonging to the Whole, which is truly fulfilling. Even parents who eschew mindless consumerism find it almost impossible to prevail against the growing trend away from Being and serenity, in favor of Having, and the angst and violence it generates.

The West claims that Islam is incompatible with democracy because it does not separate religion from politics, yet religion occupies a privileged place in

American political life. Karen Armstrong points out that the separation of church and state in America came about when Jefferson refused to anoint one of the Protestant religions. He did this so that all denominations would back the young government, whose survival was at stake. The notion that religion and government should be separate would have been incongruous in the eighteenth century, when religious belief was largely unquestioned - at least publicly. (Not to mention that the Massachusetts Bay colonies were led by their respective pastors...) As for contemporary Western intellectuals, they largely condemned religion before Islam became a problem, and now, the tree of Shari'a obscures its rich diversity of philosophical and theological thought, including the eighth century Mutazilah school, centered on reason, and Sufism that seeks oneness with the divine through chanting or whirling.

The Saudi Wahhabis, bin Laden's (and probably ISIL's) backers, are reason's latest opponents. Wahhabis, or Salafists, also condemn mysticism, as seen with the destruction of Sufi temples in Mali by Ansar Dine. As Islamic societies increasingly fall prey to Western mores, the appeal of Salafist groups such as ISIL grows, notwithstanding their brutality. At the same time, although those who look to the past with a critical and constructive spirit, who prefer books to guns, have not yet generated mass appeal, Muslim thinkers such as Tariq Ramadan are moving Islam toward a modern interpretation of the Prophet's teachings, and with varying results, voters in Egypt and Tunisia have given Islamist parties a chance to rule.

Whatever the outcome of the Arab Spring, it is clear that as a result of the critical spirit Americans have had in the past toward each of our presents, we now lack a critical spirit vis-a-vis the future to which our present points. Islamic fundamentalists go to extremes to proselytize their faith, but we have created a society that values external freedom so highly that it dismisses all notion of community and responsibility. Having yet to discover that the only real freedom is an inner state, we allow external freedom to ride roughshod over the morality that inner freedom seeks.

Because each of the three monotheistic religions have seen good and evil as absolutes, incarnated as God and the Devil, they have condemned the Other. The Christians fought the Jews more or less openly for two millennia. They fought the Muslims for a thousand years, first through crusades, then to balance the power of the Ottoman Empire, or as part of colonial conquest. The war between Islam and Judaism is a more recent one: for centuries the two peoples lived peacefully side by side in the Middle East and North Africa. The Prophet held that all ways of worshipping God were acceptable; only those who did not believe in Him were infidels.

As James Carroll shows in *Constantine's Sword,* the Jews' refusal to recognize Christ as the hoped-for Messiah stems from a strict interpretation of monotheism: God is One and indivisible, therefore he cannot have a son. Jews were the original fundamentalists, refusing to abandon a basic belief that put them at odds with Christianity. And although martyrdom represents a total renunciation of the internal authority that Jews evoked in their refusal to convert, from the Roman attack on Masada to the nineteenth century, they have repeatedly committed mass suicide to avoid it. In *The*

Battle for God, Karen Armstrong points out that Islamic culture is experiencing what Jewish culture did hundreds of years ago: modernity seen as forced conversion.

All three religions of the book fall prey to internal strife when interpretations of Truth differ. Jews have fought each other over questions of reason versus faith, and of elitism versus the needs of common people, while Christians fought over the question of direct versus mediated relations with God, and conflicting interpretations of the Qu'ran historically spawned sects, wars and assassinations. Just as the crusades and the wars of religion disrupted centuries of European and Middle Eastern life, Islam's 'Reformation' is likely to disrupt modernity as long as both sides in the struggle espouse violence instead of counter-balancing.

Both Taoism and Islam refer to a path. For Taoists, the path represents the Whole, while in Islam, it is laid out by God. For both, however, it implies responsibility. In the Judeo-Christian civilizations, rights are given by God, leaving responsibility out in the cold, while in Islam God gives no rights, but requires responsibility - or obedience. Thus the crucial difference between the two cultures is not the relationship between religion and the state, but the relative value of rights and responsibilities. Each culture also has a downside: God-given rights result in absolute external freedom, while blind obedience to God's will can lead to the sacrifice of reason. The following graph compares the three religions from the point of view of freedom and obedience, tolerance and morality.

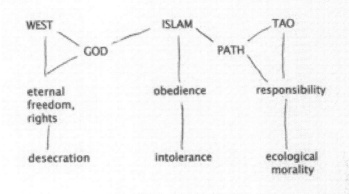

Battles both between and within religions are typical of the antagonistic situations that characterize linear, dualistic cultures. Among contemporary commentators, Fukuyama sees history turning on *thymos*, or the need for recognition, while Chomsky opposes greed to rebellion, and more recently, in *Terror and Liberalism*, Paul Berman lumps Communism, Fascism and Islam together as totalitarian regimes opposing liberalism. All these are linear, tit for tat approaches that ignore process.

The modern Muslim thinker who inspired the Salafists was Sayyid Qutb, whose strictures are increasingly echoed by critics of modernity. According to Berman, writing in the sixties, after spending two years in the United States, this Egyptian educator echoed counter-cultural writers such as Theodor Roszak, tracing modern angst to ancient Greece's commitment to reason, "the arrogant faith which in modern times produced the tyranny of technology over life." Qut'b saw modern man

> ...suffering from affliction, distress, nervous and psychological diseases, perversion, idiocy, insanity and crime. He roves without destination, killing his monotony and weariness by means that exhaust the soul, body and nerves; adopting narcotics, alcohol, dark, perverted ideas, desperate and illusive doctrines.

According to Qutb: "Even in the most affluent and advanced Western societies, people lead the most miserable lives, having lost touch with their souls." He warned against

> ...a temporary prosperity, which lasts until the natural laws have produced their effects, allowing the consequences of the split between material excellence and spiritual fulfillment to appear in full" (starting with) maldistribution, which allows hatred, grudges, misery and fear of the unexpected to take root.

For Qutb, the split between material excellence and spiritual fulfillment began with Christianity. Judaism had correctly refused to draw any distinction between the sacred and the secular, because there is only one God. Qut'b agreed that to separate them is to imply that there is more than one authority, therefore more than one God. On the other hand, when Jesus' disciples emphasized spirituality and love, they lost sight of the Mosaic code, which strictly regulated daily life. Then, in another pendulum swing, Christians countered Roman debauchery with monastic asceticism, which is at odds with human nature.

To quote Berman on Qutb again:

> The whole purpose of liberalism, originally a response to English religious wars, was to put religion in one corner and the state in another. Qutb believed

that the (Christian) separation of the secular and the
spiritual, together with the Greek reverence for rationality, is what ultimately led to the dominance of
technology. Islam's purpose, which he saw as another pendulum swing, was to establish a correct,
non-distorted relation between man and the physical world, at the same time as it reestablished the
rule of God over man's affairs.

Qutb was among those Muslim thinkers for
whom the divine spirit was also and unequivocally one
of social justice. Although it should be clear by now
that the path toward equity requires not more religion,
but more responsibility, by lessening individual internal
authority - the trusting of one's own ability to reason -
both the West's illusion of absolute freedom and Islam's
obedience to a higher power have impeded this pursuit.
Both the West and Islam need to move away from their
dualistic ethos, with its linear implications, toward recognition that humans are part of a Whole. Islam needs
to return to the Prophet's respect for internal authority,
and the West needs to realize that it is not rights that are
absolute, but the sacredness of Being. It would seem
that both societies could walk the path of life with a
modicum of serenity if they could accept the idea that
responsibility does not flow from any external Truth or
God-given freedom, but from man's only real freedom,
which is inalienable because it is internal.

Faith does not require an effort, but choosing a
path does. For both Islam and the West, the effort required to walk the path can flow from awareness of the
absolute nature of internal freedom, as opposed to the
relativity of external freedom. Responsibility dictated
by recognition of the sacredness of Being as the only
absolute, would dispose the Western world to obey the

laws it gives itself, in order to preserve its habitat. And as the Muslim world confronts the ecological imperative, obedience could be translated by, as Qut'b suggests, establishing a non-distorted relation between man and the physical world.

Narrow though this opening may be, I am suggesting that it could create a common ground upon which both cultures could move toward sustainable development for the planet. Both should be able to accept the comment of a Buddhist wise man: "Your little will can't do anything. It takes Great Determination. Great Determination doesn't mean just you making an effort. It means the whole universe is behind you and with you - the birds, the trees, the sky, the moon, and the ten directions." (Quoted by Nathalie Goldberg in *Writing Down the Bones*.)

When Islam kills and destroys in the name of God it betrays its Golden Age, when knowledge was supreme (though that Golden Age was of greater lasting benefit to the civilizations it conquered than to its indigenous populations). However it is no different from a West that kills and destroys to 'remain free'. American rulers affirm the right to exploit the entire world's wealth, exporting a culture dictated by profit, in which Freedom to Be is seen as Freedom to Have and to Do. Some not only want to 'shop til they drop', they would sacrifice their lives to remain free to do so. Is this so different from the suicide bomber who is willing to die to impose the will of God? Each side justifies killing in the name of a belief, curtailing the internal freedom that encompasses belief, one because it denies the value of individual freedom, the other because it sees freedom as an external good.

Before invading Afghanistan and Iraq, American foreign policy experts could have known that democratic elections would not solve the problem of Islamic fundamentalism, had they remembered - or been aware of - what happened in Algeria in 1992: Islamists were poised to win the first nationwide free election in the country's history; in a panic, the government, backed by France, the former colonial power, called off the planned second round of voting. During the decade that followed, thousands of people were killed by Islamic terrorists while the Algerian army stood by. More recently, in Egypt, the election of a member of the Muslim Brotherhood to the presidency ended in a military coup and the re-establishment of a regime similar to the one the short-lived Egyptian revolution ousted from power.

As for the Israeli/Palestinian conflict, the only one to have lasted during the entire period from the Second World War to the present, it stood American diplomacy on its head, as we simultaneously declared the Palestinians' right to a state, and gave Israel the means to deny it. (Both Israelis and Palestinians resorted to terrorism against Ottoman, then British rule. Menachem Begin and Yitzak Shamir, both future Prime Ministers, were active in Irgun, the main Jewish terrorist organization.) Failing to realize that this conflict would serve as a template for wars of colonial liberation across the South, the United States made it part of the play of Cold War alliances, giving it a legitimacy it should never have had, creating a template for the settling of one people on the land of another, which sooner or later results in having to relocate the intruders. And once the conservative Saudis and other Sunni oil princes realized it had become a matrix for demands for equity that could end their power, they backed the fundamentalists now wrecking havoc across the Middle East.

Two hundred years ago, the French Revolution separated political and spiritual power, and at present, without the moral content that religions once provided, the polis is sinking into barbarity. Intellectuals' repulsion for religious establishments, together with our conviction that religious dogma has been harmful to society, have prevented us from recognizing that morality need not be seen as dictated by the Otherness of God, but can be based on a concept of the Whole confirmed by science, and on the individual authority and sense of responsibility that recognition fosters.

There is growing worldwide awareness that globalization must be ecological or it will destroy the planet. Lacking is a theoretical framework based not on 'Truths', but on knowledge-based morality. I believe that if it were more widely recognized that limits are inherent in nature, most people would realize that since man is part of nature, he cannot enjoy absolute external freedom. In the North in particular, that realization could justify the limits on individual and governmental behavior that are required by the ecological imperative and sustainable development.

Alas, the acceleration of history has made us impatient. With our 'Better Dead than Red' mentality, we demand that everyone have free elections tomorrow, naively believing that would solve the world's problems. Most Muslims, however, would probably prefer a long term process of autopoietic change rather than 'heroic' death in a battle against modernity. The fervor of bearded men threatening women and infidels has been nurtured by political leaders representing highly authoritarian governments. And one would be hard pressed to affirm that Western societies are more free from external authority than were tribes-people 13,000 years ago. Marcuse was naive to believe that unfettered freedom would solve humanity's problems. Now that we have been to the moon, the re-appropriation of internal authority should be the new frontier.

As Alan Watts notes in *Man Woman and Nature*: "Man is free to the extent that he realizes his genuine self (i.e., the Atman) to be the author and origin of nature." Or, as Meister Eckhart put it in a quote which I find immensely pleasing to the intellect:

> God must be I, I very God, so consummately one that this he and this I are one 'is', in this is-ness working one work eternally; but so long as this is and this I, to wit, God and the soul, are not one single here, one single now, then I cannot work with, nor be one with that He.

Awareness of the Oneness of all things, which is not new to Islam, would foster the morality it sees lacking in our society, and from which we are the first to suffer. A circular approach to the world's staggering problems would seek solutions based on awareness that humans are part of a Whole, which, at this point in human history some call God. God is up there, humans are down here, and because they disagree on how to worship him, violence reigns.

A circular view of the situation would suggest that God, men and the universe are one, leaving little room for conflict.

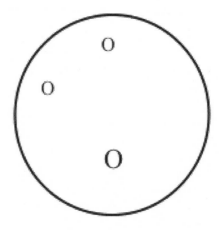

But we cannot usefully discuss violence without exploring whether it has biological roots. A useful way to go about this is to consider how human violence differs from animal violence, and how linear civilization has abetted that difference.

VI
Otherness and Violence

Renouncement and discipline
in action lead to the final goal.
But discipline is more important
than renouncement.
Bhagavad Gita

We turn now to the findings on violence of the French psychiatrist and ethologist, Boris Cyrulnik. Cyrulnik defines violence as "a point of view expressed through behaviors which fail to take into account the existence of the Other". He then goes on to show that the major difference between animal and human violence is that, in the animal world it is *perceptions* that provoke emotions. These create rituals for interactions, which in turn dictate behaviors that control violence. Quite differently, human rituals are created by our *representations* of the Other, which is why theories "can even allow the aggressor to feel like a saint when he carries out an act of purification".

In evolutionary terms, the development of the brain, which brought us abstract thinking, creativity and language, also enabled us to put other humans in a different category from ourselves, something animals do not do. In *One World,* the ethicist Peter Singer notes that massacres, and even genocide, appear to have always been part of human behavior. Today however, it is imperative for us to evolve toward Other-toleration.

The findings in Cyrulnik's *Affective Nourishment* plug directly into the situation in big city streets, the Middle East - and 9/11. "No sensory information can inhibit the behavior of a human being who has a hateful idea of the Other, since he responds to his representations rather than to his perceptions. This explains why racists are capable of destroying a ten year old girl: 'One day she would have eaten our bread!'" These are exactly the words of a Jewish boy in an Israeli documentary, approving the massacre in a Hebron mosque of children his own age. These children were seen merely in their Otherness.

Cyrulnik notes that a mouse is highly stimulating to a cat because its biological configuration (shape, way of moving, color, smell), give the cat a great deal of meaningful information.

> The cat does not represent the mouse world, and is incapable of being disturbed at the idea of eating a mother mouse, leaving several little mice orphans. It responds to a set of stimuli. Whether we are predators, commensals or parasites, it is affective indifference which authorizes us to destroy the other. And this indifference is explained by the fact that we live in non-communicable worlds.

According to Cyrulnik, animals and men process information and use cognition differently. Animals process information with their whole being, while men have driven it into a small part of their anatomy, the brain. When Cyrulnik tells us that "a present perception evokes a memory that creates internal stimuli which are like thought ambassadors," we are reminded of the centuries old hatred between Sunni and Shia. For Cyrulnik: "It is surely our aptitude to live in a world of representations that created our aptitude for violence, at the same time as it created our aptitude for culture." For Cyrulnik, as for Sade, a culture that did away with all human violence would no longer be creative. But while Sade lauds violence, Cyrulnik regrets the fact that 20th century civilization has been unable to control it, abasing its culture.

Cyrulnik believes that men are violent because they are determined to eliminate those who live in a different representation, and that contact dissipates violence by re-establishing an exchange of emotions. From the advent of chiefs and priests to the time when the village constituted an individual's entire world, it was easier to have a close relationship with one's neighbors, and that world was a manageable - if not comfortable - place. When immigrants live in ghettos, without representation in the minds of the former inhabitants, contact fails to happen and homes are set on fire.

But is man not also compelled to destroy a human, accessible 'Other', because he cannot destroy the Supreme Other, to whom, in the end, he must bow in death? Does not our representation of the Other pass through our representation of God, who is irrevocably in a different world of representation from the one we are in ourselves? A foreign world of representation which ricochets back to us at the sight of a human Other? Cyrulnik tells us that we have to find some middle ground between animal rituals that prevent violence, allowing us to recognize each other and confront our respective rituals, and hegemonic rituals that provoke violence. Examples of modern rituals are philosophical debates, scientific revues and round tables.

> Through debate, masturbation ceased to be frowned upon, homosexuality became better accepted among certain social classes, and feminists improved the condition of women without killing a single man or setting off a single bomb. Unfortunately, the disadvantage of this type of solution is that it leads to uncertainty. To be reassured, we need the illusion of an overarching truth.

According to Cyrulnik, small groups use debates to modify mentalities and social structures, exchange taking on different ritual forms according to the number of participants. "In a couple or a family, emotion triggered by arguments is difficult to manage because affective proximity bars rituals. The intervention of an outsider makes discussion possible by ritualizing it." The creation of gangs corresponds to the same need as the belief in God:

> Equidistant from too much closeness, which authorizes family violence, and too much distance, which leads to social violence, small groups structured around ideas, action and affects constitute a human-sized organization, in which the individual can easily personalize himself through affective and intellectual exchange.A small group or tribe gathering several families that worship an affective, intellectual or existential totem, constitutes the most basic fight against anomy.

One could say that rituals are an antidote to linear, or tit for tat behavior. When needs are met through rituals, they become more circular, fused with the needs and urges of other participants, tending toward outcomes rather than requiring results. Commenting on the fact that medieval man lived out his life in a homogeneous community, Cyrulnik adds:

> A world without rituals is a raw world, reduced to matter, weight and measures, while a ritualized world instills history into things, gives them meaning and allows for togetherness. Ours is a disintegrated world, in which de-solidarized individuals run into each other, meet each other or argue according to their urges and needs. A ritualized world links individuals with each other harmoniously, creating a social body, a group to which they belong and which reassures them.

Cyrulnik mentions that the first study of a de-ritualized society was carried out among the Iks, who were deported to a beautiful region and given government pensions, with nothing to worry about. "With no project and no history, they lost their social ties, and in a few months, their relations turned violent. The brutal destruction of their lifestyle put them at the degree zero of humanity. They began to hurt each other, steal food, rape, abandon their children and leave their dead unburied." All other things being equal, is this not what is happening in overdeveloped societies, where atomization is the norm? Does it truly make sense to negate people's need for community because it could foster inter-community violence? Is such violence not in part the outcome of the psychological violence done to children in one-parent families that affects the basic fabric of personality?

Recent research in the U.S. shows that the failure to achieve total integration is due in part to a widespread preference for living and studying among one's own kind. That people should seek to live amongst like folk may also be less a matter of intolerance than a reaction to the stress of impersonal mega-cities. (That we live surrounded by strangers in our housing arrangements is, come to think of it, properly mind-boggling.)

Even small towns have been increasingly shorn of their essence. As Qut'b pointed out half a century ago, we drag our loneliness to suburban malls, which offer not only greater economic choice, but also an illusion of pleasure instead of the more tangible pleasures derived from the human interactions that flourish in towns and neighborhoods. How not to recognize in our call for rituals the enduring need for community?

> At a time when culture no longer impregnates the inter-human world, clan rituals preserve a bit of their archaic affectivity. And those who love each other unite in hatred, right before total de-ritualization, where it is 'each man for himself' and society is pulverized. In groups of abandoned street children, archaic rituals unite through the violence imposed on the Other, such as fights or group robberies. But there are also interactive rituals, such as affective exchanges, to becalm and put to sleep.

At the end of the nineteenth century, when Western societies had not yet acquired their modern structures, Durkheim suggested the concept of anomy to describe human groups that no longer have natural or legal forms. Cyrulnik wonders whether the resurgence of anomy at the end of the 20th century means that the destructuring of almost all societies is paving the way for a new human order of the type portrayed in *the Hunger Games*. One of the foremost problems raised by futurists is population growth. In megalopolises, social groups become incapable of creating cultural evolution other than through violence. No wonder attempted suicides and road accidents are no longer news, that drugs and AIDS, which have become cultural stars, symbolize the destructive needs of today's youth.

As Cyrulnik emphasizes, at this stage of personal development, the incentive to life is outside the family. And because the outside is empty (i.e., full of Others...), solutions are mainly cultural. As an example he mentions the crucial role of tradition in North Africa: "When the Ramadan brings back the rituals, with their daily family and friendly encounters, the suicide rate drops instantly. In the West, our cultural impotence is illustrated by the fact that depression and suicide rates climb at Christmas and on Mother's Day." Is not Bin Laden saying in a destructive way what Cyrulnik is saying in a constructive way about modernity?

In the North, while violence against immigrants is about visceral fear of the 'Other', gang wars are about Having. In the South violence is about denying the Other his inherent - or potential - power over a territory. According to Cyrulnik:

> The world of signs created a new mental order in which all violence is possible, since every freedom is possible: not only that of destroying one rule to propose another, but also a person or group that gets in the way of that rule, in the name of the idea we have of them or the threat they represent. An animal, on the other hand, is always immersed in a relationship between an organism and a thing. Even if he organizes stimulations so as to transform them into intelligent representations, this does not sufficiently remove him from the context to eliminate the regulating effect of rituals that control emotions. Animal violence is born from an alteration of the laws of nature, while human violence is born from their transgression in words and civility.

Cyrulnik's "biological aptitude to pull ourselves out of a context and invent signs", are among the human characteristics that have reduced our perception of being part of the Whole. Hegemonic rituals are one means by which we are persuaded to relinquish our internal authority, and our aptitude for culture allows us to formalize that renunciation. Only spontaneous ritualization brings us closer to the Other:

> It is the ritualization of words which enables us to assimilate emotionally a face to face encounter. As proof, in conversation we position our bodies before ex-changing words; as in any true ritual, each gesture of the body structures an emotional exchange. Words are always accompanied by a distribution of affects: I am silent when you speak, I look away in order not to trouble you, you nod to encourage me, etc. All these behavioral scenarios manage the emotions brought out by our words. Conversation, certainly the most human of our acts, creates a sensory area which is structured like a ritual. During a conversation, our affects are exchanged at the same time as we tell stories which spell out our identities.

Clinical experience shows that a person hits out if he cannot speak. "It is the act that prevails and has the value of words. When in a relationship between two people, one person is unable to express himself, or the other does not allow him to, or when institutions fail to create places for exchange, acts destroy the Other and all thought as well." It is easy enough to set off a ritual between two people, or in a small group. But when there are masses of people or over-population, order can only take shape under a dictatorship, that governs without discussion through administrative violence (Laszlo's selective disregard). Unless a culture invents the right code, in which men can express themselves and govern without destroying other humans. This code is called tolerance, and Cyrulnik believes we can learn to decenter ourselves with respect to our own thoughts, admitting there is more than one way to be a human being.

Cyrulnik tells us that: "As long as we despise the other, we will oscillate between the violence of disorder and that of a unique order. As long as we have civilization to invent, we shall create violence, since we will have to destroy the old laws." The only civilizations that have succeeded in evolving by managing violence are those that instituted disruptions - in other words, phase transitions - that blunt antagonisms. At this point in human evolution, autopoiesis requires us to learn from and adapt to, the Other.

To enlarge our discussion of Otherness we shall take a closer look at external authority, incarnated in the sovereignty of nations, self-appointed guardians of civilization.

VII
Otherness and Sovereignty

Of the King it is said that his frontiers
extend to the sky's orbit. His countries
are gathered in a single beam in his hand.
Egypt is everywhere he is. He gathered
the universality of beings in his grasp.
Amenophis's stele at Guiza

Twenty-first century fundamentalism underscores the diminished power of state sovereignty, while democracy implies the right of minority groups to create their own state. Although the behavior of nations is intimately linked to the exercise of authority, economic power is increasingly borderless. The concept of allegiance, the survival of the Nation-state and the future of governance come under this triple constraint.

Nature and God have always been the outstanding Others. In prehistoric times, the immediate Other was a member of the same clan who competed for available food, shelter and women. The Supreme Other was the strongest, bravest male. Neighboring groups were more distant Others, and each fought to preserve its territory. When the distances between groups increased, their ways of speaking diverged and they became not only Other, but potentially antagonistic strangers. As battles involved ever larger groups, fortified cities were built, governed by the princes who owned the surrounding land and led the men in battle.

For a long time, the relationship between the many who served and the one who led was a direct one. The clan chief was first among equals. When clans evolved into tribes, then states, the wealth gleaned from tribute set chiefs, then princes, above their subjects. The renunciation of inner authority had already begun when God became the Supreme Other, and when a prince became king, he incarnated the Supreme Otherness of God, becoming thrice removed from the many. Land belonged to The King, and as long as he remained the strongest male, princes though fighting his battles (which were also God's), could only govern portions of it. From the Middle Ages to the triumph of absolutism, the authority of kings was challenged by that of the princes, who now owed him allegiance only in war. Finally, when kings found themselves caught between princely defiance and the internationalism of the church, theoreticians of absolute royal power pushed through the separation of Church and State, making kings 'sovereign' and limiting the power of the Pope.

By limiting the sovereignty of the church, that is, God, kings consolidated their sovereignty over their subjects. The power they derived from God now served to introduce the concept of Nation, increasing yet further the distance between rulers and subjects: though not a person, but a concept, the nation commanded the same allegiance as a king. Although personally unaffected by the Otherness of the nation's enemies, subjects were compelled to fight them. The difference between clan violence and state violence is that the former was carried out against an entire society's enemies, while the enemies of the state, like those of the king, are 'virtual' to those who die fighting them.

Space determines the definition of both 'otherness' and 'sovereign'. Thus, in addition to supreme authority, or the power to rule, sovereignty implies the separateness of states. Whether it be an autocracy or a democracy, a country's sovereignty only exists to the extent that there are other sovereignties with which it can interact. A sovereign entity deals only with its equals: only a state can enter into negotiations with another state, and that is how it exercises the sovereignty that protects its Otherness.

As men realized the strength of numbers, society moved from the challenges of individual competitors for power, to those of the many against the few - a struggle for economic sovereignty, or freedom. The French Revolution revived the Greek concept of democracy, under which 'the citizens' were sovereign, and could remove the king. However it took another two hundred years for sovereignty to pass to that group of citizens that was larger than any other. By then, internal authority had been reduced to an 'I' which, no longer involved in self-making, had allowed its relations with 'the Other' to be regulated by the external authority of the state.

Sovereignty is the most powerful embodiment of external authority, and is the exclusive attribute of those who govern, whether by force or delegation. Even in a modern democracy, notwithstanding soothing words, and although they elect their rulers, citizens are often opposed to the decisions they take. Furthermore, they cannot be sovereign with respect to other nations because they lack the corresponding vis a vis which alone gives sovereignty its meaning: the people of one country do not negotiate with the people of another, but can only face them in combat.

When democracy removed sovereignty from the hands of the monarch and gave it to 'the people', it brought the notion of Otherness much closer to home. He, or those, to whom the individual submits is by definition 'Other', but now the Other is no longer only the king in his castle, but potentially all those who belong to another group. And notwithstanding democracy's claim to universalism, the Otherness of the majority can become a form of tyranny. At its most benign it requires the minority to respect its will (you shall do this because it is what most people think is best). And while proclaiming freedom of expression, the temptation is almost irresistible to hem in the minority's right to be heard, in its most acute form preventing it from forming its own sovereign state.

The battles for independence increasingly being waged by various 'small peoples' who, in a multinational state are destined to be minorities, express a refusal to accept tyranny under the cloak of universalism. Many of these peoples reaffirm universalism as the timeless political ideal from which public life flows, and which is inalienable, like the 'God given' rights referred to in the American constitution. But states have difficulty accepting that universalism must also protect that which differentiates one people from another. Ethnic or religious minorities have no specific rights other than the system of checks and balances that protect all individuals from government.

Universalism, which we could call 'Ground', constitutes the basis upon which civil rights are erected, and is the indispensable foundation of civil peace. Since it can be put into practice just as well in ethnically homogeneous countries such as Japan or Hungary, as in melting pot societies, and since all democratic republics are alike to the extent that they share the same universality - the only differences between them being, precisely, ethnic or religious - the people's right to choose their form of government should imply the right of ethnic and religious minorities to set up independent states. Surely, groups who share a common history, geography, language, customs (or any of the things that distinguish it from another group and sooner or later lead to war), are entitled to live together under the rule of the strongest among them (referred to as their 'elected leaders'). How then can we demand that they blur those ethnic or religious traditions that distinguish them from others in the name of the universality they share with them? If states choose a republican form of government, universal basic principles will prevail, but whether they do so is an internal affair, to be decided on a democratic basis. If a country is not democratic, then the question is, do other nations have the right to intervene? Outsiders hesitate to rescue civilians from civil conflicts because that would infringe upon the sovereignty of the states involved, yet the fact that ad hoc groups can inflict serious damage upon states makes sovereignty all but meaningless.

In a world made up of kings and princes, it was imperative to move beyond feudalism to some semblance of unity in order for society to progress. In the twenty-first century, progress lies in ungluing the pieces on one level, and gluing them together on another, that of decentralized, local democracy. Political analysts warn that we are entering a new Middle Ages, yet in a sense we need to reinvent the internationalism of that time, replacing the notion of the universal republic derived from the authority of kings, with that of a republic of *gens* derived from individual internal authority.

We shall discuss the relationship between internal authority and freedom further on. Here we need to digress a moment on that between economic progress, identity, and freedom. All notions of freedom imply limits, and when Marcuse focused on the issue of whether freedom was a public or private affair, he missed the essential: both individual and public freedom are limited by the Other's freedom. When we say 'my freedom stops where my neighbor's begins', we are talking about individual limits. When we say 'my country's freedom stops where another country's freedom begins', we are talking about sovereign limits. I call freedom associated with space, and with peace or conflict, *lateral freedom*. But freedom or its lack can also be linked to the power of the few over the many with respect to the latter's economic conditions, and this I call *vertical freedom*.

During the 19th century, in the name of universalism, various peoples, valuing economic progress over identity, were willing to forego a measure of lateral freedom and unite within nation-states. Since then, in the developed world at least, basic economic rights have been enshrined, and men no longer have to sacrifice their identity to lateral domination in order to achieve vertical freedom. This has resulted in a multitude of efforts to restore the lateral freedom that is embodied in independent states, whether by groups within a state (such as the Catalans), or inhabiting a territory they consider to be their own (such as the Serbs). The universalism that acted as a bootstrap a hundred years ago is valid at present solely when all groups consider economic progress more important than identity.

Unfortunately, political establishments have yet to accept the idea of replacing national parliaments by a global parliament to which power is delegated in recognition of the limits of national sovereignty. Yet it should be clear that the decline of the Nation-state requires two levels of democracy, local and global; one for freedom and the other for peace, both representing horizontal limits. As globalization stands today, sovereign countries are ever less able to solve their respective economic problems alone. Economic chaos cries out for worldwide reform, while catastrophes, be they wars or the increasing number of natural disasters caused by climate change, show the need for full-time peace-keeping and humanitarian aid directorates. Together with the allocation of resources on a worldwide basis and the regulation of financial markets, global coordination can go far toward reviving small communities, limiting the sovereignty of individual states to the right to levy taxes and declare war.

Christ lived and preached in a small community at a time when there was no internet, yet eventually, his message reached the entire world. Today, with an eye to fame (the epitome of Having), fewer people live in small communities in which they can invest themselves in a variety of roles, where each is known to all, with their respective abilities, merits and limitations. In the final analysis, nations consist of groups of individuals linked on an occasional basis by proximity, class, sex, age, and profession, rather than by language, custom, history or geography, which together gave rise to frontiers.

It is because the nation commands less allegiance than the group, that even under the most efficient systems, states have become impossible to govern. The need is for democratically wielded power to be returned to the local, immediate environment, and to the neighbors, classes, age groups, sexes, and professions within it. The nation-state would then become the intermediary between global governance and local government, a relay translating into a local legislative framework the decisions taken on a world level, which must partly dictate what actions may be safely undertaken on a local level. (Those who deal with the big picture would rotate in order not to lose touch with local realities.)

There is one more thing that needs to be said with respect to sovereignty: it must not be confused with allegiance. On one side are national decision makers, who are sovereign vis à vis their counterparts in other nations, and on the other are subjects, who owe them allegiance. When states join together, as in the European Union, there arises a question of sovereignty of last resort, which refers not only to the power of governments to make decisions vis à vis other governments, but also to the citizen's obligation to obey them.

It is precisely in questions of last resort that the citizen's allegiance is crucial: without it, there can be no state. Hence, when a group of states decides to unite, allegiance must pass from each individual state to the mega-state. For how can a state which no longer mints money, commands its own army or raises taxes constitute the principal seat of sovereignty, that of relations with other sovereignties that commands last resort allegiance? In the event of war between the European Union and a country outside it, citizens would have to obey the Union, otherwise it would cease to exist.

The Otherness that evolved from chief, to prince, to king, to nation, is today ever more abstract - and ever greater. As nations have become weaker, their power challenged by other entities, whether multi-nationals or terrorists, the threat posed by Otherness has become as acute as in the most primitive of times - or the most authoritarian. The North clings to the illusion of the absolute sovereignty of its Nation-states, with the United States, the most powerful, distant Other playing a role similar to that of kings in the past vis a vis princes. In the South nation-building is increasingly threatened, as peoples fight to secede from the Nation-states to which they have been assigned by colonial powers, refusing to share their (so-called) sovereignty with 'Others', who belong to different tribes, speak a different language and obey their own charismatic male.

The United States is no more likely to relinquish its power than a king, but it, too, can lose it by violent means. And if September 11th has taught us anything, it is that attitudes toward death play a major role in what is happening to the world-as-system.

VIII
Death Denied, Death Defied

This is the word which was in darkness.
Every luminous spirit that knows it will
be among the living.
Egyptian Coffin Texts

The search for the meaning of life often boils down to the question: 'Why must I die?', implying that if life does not go on forever, it has no meaning. No individual life goes on forever, because life as a physical phenomenon must alternate with death. However, because it is the Whole, or Being, that is meaningful, rather than power or action, we do not need to seek meaning outside ourselves, in an accumulation of acts accomplished and recognized by an external authority. Life itself does not have an ultimate meaning, but everything that occurs as part of Being contributes to our individual meaning.

When two commercial jets were rammed into the World Trade Towers, the West was confronted with a terrifying fact: people can be made to believe that their death will be a ticket to paradise, and that the deaths of others are inconsequential in the service of a supreme Other. When considering this and other atrocities, it may be useful to explore overall societal attitudes toward death and how they evolved.

I believe we fear death because it alone escapes the power of the supreme external authority. And because external authority leads to a morality that views freedom as an absolute, and Having as more important than Being, the ways in which we court and mete out death are related to both. Terrorist attacks do not show that there is a greater willingness to die violently in the South than in the North, but merely that the motivations are different. While in the Islamic world some are still ready to die for God, it was not so long ago that the cry 'For God and country' resonated in the Western world.

Perhaps partly due to the way death has been portrayed on film for several generations, members of affluent societies are willing to risk death for both abstract and material reasons: to 'remain free', or for criminal gain. Paradoxically, in those same societies, few people plan for death beyond making a will; the idea of deciding the moment of one's own demise is only slowly being accepted. Indeed, our desire to abolish all constraints has led to a Promethean determination to vanquish death. Desperate medical interventions are not so much about achieving immortality as about refusing the ultimate defeat.

Yet longevity, which often leads to cancer, and medical progress, which allows us to prolong life even when it consists mainly of suffering, increasingly result in a patient - or his family - begging the medical profession for release. While the rich or well insured can prolong their lives for years, others die of starvation, avoidable disease and fixable injuries. Some years ago *The Economist* affirmed that soon we will die when someone else decides it. Meanwhile, the rich in the North cling to life at any cost, even if this means that the children of the South go uncared for.

In modern societies, death is not only fearful because it involves suffering, it is unacceptable because it is The-End-of-the-Self-As-a-Thing-We-Have. When the American colonists coined the phrase 'the right to life, liberty and the pursuit of happiness', they were referring to vertical freedom defined in the preceding chapter. Today, the 'right to life' movement makes death seem almost unnatural. Like the notion of sovereignty, its meaning has been distorted, and it is now interpreted not only as the fetus's inherent right to become a viable child, but as the right to fight death ...to the death, no matter how futile and what the cost to others. We have confused that which can be the object of law and morality, i.e., the social sphere, with a fact of nature, 'that which is'. Believers call this divine will. I prefer to call it the order of things, as expressed in the second chapter.

A few people are beginning to affirm that all deaths are not equal; that the death of a sixty year old is less regrettable than that of a child or youth, because the latter have had no chance 'to enjoy life'. Yet anyone suggesting that medical research be concentrated on children and youth is accused of murderous designs on the elderly. Allowing an old person to die is seen as a greater crime than killing a young person, for the simple reason that we shall all be old some day, while we shall never be young again. Old people have 'worked hard all their lives', therefore they are entitled to live 'the rest of their lives' as long as medically possible. One cannot help but wonder how many aspects of life would be different if death were not considered its supreme enemy.

According to Stuart Kauffman, far from being a fluke, life "was bound to evolve from the simple, profound transformation of dead molecules. It is a natural property of complex chemical systems, no matter which chemicals are involved, and it is from their diversity that life springs." Thus, life - and death - are 'how things are', and do not require the intervention of a Supreme Other (or, in Kauffman's words, a master choreographer). When the Hindus say '*tat tvam asi*', 'that art thou', they are saying that each life partakes of the Whole-that-is. Once we understand the order and disorder of the Whole - or life- we can accept death as part of its ever-changing, dynamic processes.

Our relationship to death goes far toward explaining our relationship to religion. For the American Indians, the Buddhists and Taoists, death is merely a change of worlds, part of a natural cycle, while in the religions of the book, death is linked to the concept of a Supreme Other who is outside the world of men and to whom they must bow. Islamists tout martyrdom, while Christians join them in expecting rewards in heaven. (Some will argue that the Judeo-Christian fear of death fostered progress, but progress turns out to be a mixed blessing when it has no limits.)

Our relationship to death also depends on whether we understand that as part of the natural order, absolute external freedom does not exist. Living things - including humans - are constrained by the needs and processes of other living things and their habitat, the limits inherent in the on-going process of life, the endless interplay of order and disorder. There is no pleasure without the portent of pain, no greater psychological pain than the anticipation of death, and no more eloquent reality than death following from life.

While in a non-dualistic world the relationship between pleasure and pain is a complementary one, in the Judeo-Christian world, dualism enshrined life as a supreme right, seeing death as an individual tragedy, subject only to 'the will of God', seen as above and hence outside of the Whole. Ironically, sharing the linear view of life of those who bow to God, the Atheist Marcuse could not see that freedom is limited. Convinced that Utopia would follow from an end to repression and domination, he failed to realize that Utopia and repression are part of the Whole, as are life and death. For Marcuse, man had to be free to indulge in the pleasure principle, period. (Linear concepts are always followed by a period.) Accusing death of working against his ideals, he equated it with domination, in a world in which man's role is to dominate nature. And he saw power's "silent, institutional agreement' with death" as proof that it is a useful instrument of repression, accusing theologians and philosophers of "turning a biological fact into an ontological essence."

But death *is* an ontological category! It enjoins us to recover the internal authority that makes human beings unique among living things, with the freedom to die when and how we choose. At the same time it tells us that because death is an intrinsically individual phenomenon, killing others to solve problems ignores the fact that 'problems' result from processes in which humans are but one element. I shall uphold here the Oriental view of death as part of process, incompatible with Marcuse's appeal to the triumph of Eros and the glorification of the individual as 'Supreme Self'.

To understand why Freud's insight about pleasure and pain was followed by Marcuse's call for an end to constraints, including those imposed by society in the name of freedom, we shall turn to the work of a French historian who saw the problem in formation. Reading Philippe Ariès' *Western Attitudes Toward Death*, we realize how far we have come, not only from the Middle Ages to the twenty-first century, but even from the time, forty years ago, when both he and Marcuse were writing. Aries foresaw the present ethos, in which increasingly men are claiming the right to 'a dignified death', as opposed to its over-medicalization. But the central thesis of his work is that sex and death were both affected by nature's all powerfulness. For thousands of years, Aries notes, man progressed by fighting nature, seeing it as a more or less hostile element to be maintained outside the society he was building. But this rampart had two weak points: love and death, "through which a bit of nature's savage violence continued to seep out".

At the end of the Middle Ages "a dangerous, wild continent emerged, bringing destructiveness to the collective consciousness." (This attitude is mirrored in fundamentalist Islam. In Jason Burke's book *Al Qaeda*, Qut'b describes women as "flirtatious, provocative, with thirsty lips and bulging breasts".) According to Aries, (as Freud emphasized, and as Marcuse was later to lament): "Our defensive system consisted of morality and religion, the building of the city and the codifying of law; the creation of an economy, organized work, collective discipline and eventually, technology, with periodic feasts briefly allowing desire, pleasure and even violence to penetrate society." (Interestingly, in some civilizations, interdictions are suspended when death occurs, however in the West death has always been closely guarded.)

Ariès tells us that in the Middle Ages, society was able to attenuate the violence of life and the aggressiveness of death by containing the first within a series of interdictions, and ritualizing the second. Alas, just as death had almost been tamed, the order of life, as opposed to the disorder of nature, was broken:

> The old continuity between life and death, a circular concept which had been part of holistic man, gave way to a series of discontinuities, as dualism became dominant, allowing the soul to survive while the body returned to dust. This changed death from an almost anonymous community affair, one of several life passages, not much more dramatic than the others, to the end and abridgment of an individual life.

In the Middle Ages, when wealth was rare, every individual had a destiny which he could not and did not want to change. But soon the rich and powerful, who were also literate, began to consider that each person had an individual biography, made up of good and bad acts, that would contribute to the final judgement. They also 'had' beloved persons, things, and fame. "By the end of the Middle Ages, the conscience of oneself and one's biography became one with the love of Having."

Even then, death continued to be a relatively natural cycle, "until man began to attribute to nature a demiurgic quality rivaling with God". When Protestant reformism brought "a great cleansing of feelings, reason and morality", man's imagination produced the first cracks in what had been a reassuring system. Even so, until the eighteenth century, men were not really afraid of death. It was a serious matter, an important, grave moment, but people didn't have to pretend it didn't exist (or falsify its appearance on television), because anxiety was channeled into familiar rituals. But just as man was enlarging the frontiers of technology and organization in order to dominate nature, "natural savagery burst upon the city he had built. In its effort to conquer nature and the environment, society had abandoned its old defenses against sex and death, and nature, whom it thought it had vanquished, reappeared and made man into a savage."

Aries' emphasis on this notion appears particularly insightful today. When we view the planet, the evolution of societies and individual lives as processes, we see that conflict is an intrinsic part of life. But Marcuse's cry for freedom renewed a trend that began in the 18th century, with Sade's perverted fantasies, as quoted by Aries:

> Each time we indulge in sterile eroticism, or cooperate with nature's assassinations (eroticism and torture being two ways for man and nature to communicate), we are certain to please her and to be acting according to her wishes, for she desires the complete annihilation of living creatures in order to have the pleasure of creating new ones.

Sade understood that death as a final state is an idea invented by man: "When matter is deprived of the sublime portion which gives it movement, it is not destroyed, but merely debased... Death provides nourishment to the earth, regenerating the animal and vegetable reigns." He also believed that unjust things were indispensable to the maintenance of the universe, "which would be troubled by an equitable order." But having understood that life and death are indispensable to one another, Sade perversely rationalized that moral laws were an attempt to go against nature. With far-reaching consequences, he affirmed that instinct, like nature, was 'beyond good and evil', and that justice was not an eternal, immutable principle for all times and places, as religion has always maintained, but depended upon human conditions, characters and temperaments.

The idea that the elements of a pair of opposites are complementary, and that nature destroys in order to create is consistent with the Oriental cycle of birth and death; but Sade degraded his intuition in the name of absolute freedom. The virtuous circle was lost, and what was passed on was Sade's perversion, which, in the hands of less subtle thinkers, led to Hiroshima.

The 'natural' goal of Sade's followers was the satisfaction of their desires, whatever the cost to others. As Potocki put it: "Pity, filial piety, tenderness, love, the indulgence of Kings, are merely refinements of egotism." Nietzsche's Superman was followed by Hegel, who advocated a superstate, prefiguring Fascism. Marcuse, who fled the Nazi state, but echoed Sade as much as he denied Nietzsche and Hegel, advocated a return to absolute freedom in the name of a higher level of society. Following on the flower children who heeded him, we now have skinheads who would agree with Sade, as they put the finishing touches to Ariès' man-as-savage. Sade's remark that "there has always been something interesting and sublime in everything that is violent in nature, which explains why children, who are closer to nature, manifest a spontaneous ferocity which society has not yet vanquished," is an apt description of post-Marcusian youth.

But how can we in the North vanquish youth's childish ferocity when society, while piously condemning its need for drugs, encourages it to fulfill its every wish? Skinheads are brought up with TV, where humans evolving on a plastic set present a fanciful image of death. A motorcycle is the hero's mount: If you die on one, you are 'living'. And if you strike down an old lady for the few dollars in her bag, you are meeting a need. The reasons for which TV characters die are no more noble than the reasons for which child viewers kill their schoolmates. Not to mention the internet and electronic games, in which killing is the primary activity.

In the South, entire peoples are being sacrificed to a modernization loosely basted onto ancient tribalism. There, death has both the old and new rationales, viewed as part of life, yet meted out to the Other, who gives his allegiance to a different charismatic leader. The schizophrenic quality of death in a South that no longer 'Is' yet does not yet 'Have', is epitomized by adolescents armed with sticks, naked according to tribal rites, or dressed as drag queens, facing peacekeepers and their machine guns with frenzied bravado. Arab culture did not have a Sade, yet Al Qaeda. while believing it combats everything Sade stood for, bought into his perversion. This suggests that the problem is absoluteness itself, rather than any particular exemplary.

Ariès points out that in the Middle Ages, it was the feeling of being a failure that was associated with death, and the Muslim world's failure to modernize may partly account for the readiness of its youth to die violently. In a North increasingly able to Have, the refusal of death is no longer primarily related to the loss of Things, but to our inability to completely dominate nature. In earlier times, children witnessed the painful death of animals and humans within the family circle, and according to Aries, we need to accept suffering in order for it to be tamed.

As rituals gave way to hygiene, making death seem repugnant, the medical profession redoubled its efforts to clean it up and eliminate suffering. As a result, the community feels less involved in a member's death, abandoning its sense of solidarity to institutions, where "fear of upsetting the dying has done away with the beauty of last moments". In fact, neither the individual nor the community are capable of shouldering death, leading to a massive confession of impotence: denying the existence of a scandalous state of affairs we can do nothing about, we behave as though it didn't exist. But far from doing away with the fear death inspires, denial has opened the way for institutionalized death, with its tubes and machines, "barbaric, more terrifying than the ghouls of the Middle Ages, and as horrible as death on the street."

What is the common denominator in attitudes toward death between North and South? If we consider the elements reviewed by Ariès together with recent trends, it appears that notwithstanding vast cultural and developmental differences, what has applied to Christian Europe and America can be laid like a decalcomania over the animist, Oriental, and even the Muslim South.

The North witnessed the development of individual death and the end of death as a community affair in the Middle Ages. The South is witnessing it now, loss of community being the greatest upheaval it has undergone in the name of modernization. Wealth became a social factor in the North in the Middle Ages; in the South it is rapidly becoming one, as atomization follows upon the heels of urbanization. Interestingly, the end of evil is one factor that still does not have the same weight in the South as in the North: in animist and Oriental cultures, evil is relativized as the other face of good, an integral part of religious belief, without the Messianic need to do something about it. In Islamic cultures, it is condemned in capital letters as an unacceptable aspect of progress, while in the North, it simply fell by the wayside in the wake of progress.

Each of these attitudes is linked to man's relationship to nature. In the North, the divorce was consummated three hundred years ago, while in the South it is happening now. In animist cultures, death was normal, and people feared it no more than did Christians in the Middle Ages. At least until the advent of television, it was seen as a painful event by the millions who on a daily basis faced natural and man-made catastrophes. However their societies are moving in a new direction, in which freedom has become an external good, and men are willing to risk Being in order to Have.

Thus far, unable to totally dominate death, Western man has rejected it, while Muslim fundamentalists have sublimated it in heroic acts which, like defeating it, are a bid to achieve the unachievable. Marcuse was convinced that as long as society maintained surveillance and punishment, progress would never lead to happiness. Railing against death's eternal link with suffering and pity, illustrated by the Romantics' embellishment of it, he was convinced that suffering was no longer an intrinsic part of the human condition, as most religions claimed, but was limited to the few deviations that morality and politics had yet to overcome. Like war and crime, death could be eliminated, if only men would refuse repression.

Although the end of repression has not led to happiness, in the twenty-first century, death is pretty much the only great fear that remains (the project of eliminating war and crime - or disorder - is part of our refusal to accept it.). Ariès suggests that we humanize death, accepting its inevitability without being ashamed of it, while avoiding a return to pain and suffering. Yet his 'aristocratic solution' that sees death as "a discrete, dignified, peaceful exit, a biological passage which has no negative meaning and is no longer feared," misses the point that death is part of life. Acceptance of death's inevitability as a manifestation of our belonging to the Whole, rather than as mercy or punishment, would be more useful to our goal of a better society and a peaceful world.

If, as Marcuse believed, men fail to resist external authority because they know they are going to die, it is because of the way we have been taught to regard death. When death is divorced from life, we are convinced that freedom is outside ourselves, and can be obtained by defeating repression. But the call for freedom from death cannot be answered: instead, it turns sex and violence into a desperate substitute, degrading society. If death were understood as part of life, and freedom considered as internal rather than external, I believe that oppression would loose a great deal of its force, and sex and violence would return to their place as part of the order/disorder that is life.

Before modern medicine, once a person contracted a fatal disease, death came swiftly. Although disorder, or entropy, must ultimately win out, death need not be preceded by a maximum of suffering. Instead of the medical establishment trying to ward it off as long as possible with palliative measures that only underscore the patient's impotence, when a fatal condition occurs, doctors should lay out choices in terms of treatment - and cessation thereof. Emphasis should be on enabling the person to do the things he or she wants to do before dying, allowing her to choose insofar as possible the time and mode of death, rather than staving it off as long as possible, alive mainly to anxiety and suffering. The transformation would begin with the way we refer to our own death. Unless it comes at an early age, instead of announcing to friends and relatives: "I'm dying", as if we were the victim of a catastrophe that could have been avoided, we would inform them, as humans used to do, that: "The end of my life is near". The Taoists have it right when they affirm that only premature death is a tragedy.

The hospice movement is a generous one. But it involves a protracted effort to get the patient to accept death, while doing the utmost to relieve a suffering that still must be borne ('on a scale of one to ten'), refusing to allow the patient to die until the pain can no longer be mitigated. If, like Marcuse, we want to abbreviate suffering, we should weigh the legions of elderly hooked up to sophisticated life-prolonging devices - a growing percentage of the population of the developed world - against the tens of thousands of children in developing countries who die before the age of five.

Often, the walking-dead in old age homes point out that they have no other choice but to go on living. We've been taught to value choice, but when it comes to dying, we bow to obey external authority. Is not accepting to die as society dictates the ultimate abandonment of internal authority? The development of Reason that could have led to a full recognition of Self led instead to a rejection of Being and a loss of Self. It is unlikely that Marcuse's political exhortations penetrated the establishment, however his rantings on death fell upon receptive ears across the political spectrum.

In this chapter, we may appear to have left the question of spirituality behind; in reality, it was to better apprehend it that we have analyzed Otherness, sovereignty and death. We must now ask ourselves whether the remarkable willingness to die violently in both North and South follows from an existential despair, or perhaps, from the view of freedom as external to self.

IX
Freedom, Otherness and the Absolute

For what can ecosystems, political systems,
have in common? The wonderful possibility
that on many fronts, life evolves toward a
regime that is poised between order and chaos.
Stuart Kauffman

With the help of various thinkers, I've inventoried the major elements of the present world crisis: the violence associated with our intolerance of Otherness, issues of sovereignty, attitudes toward death, and our obsession with Having as opposed to Being. It's time now to suggest that these may be related to the spiritual quest about which so much is being said and written, after a century of intellectual atheism and agnosticism. In the remaining chapters we'll continue our discussion of the effect circular thinking could have on the problématique, returning to the notions introduced in chapter two, as the concept of sacredness leads us from evolution and biology into quantum physics and geography.

With all that science has taught us, ever fewer people believe in something that challenges common sense, but most fail to wonder whether skepticism must necessarily deprive us of serenity. I will argue that spirituality can flow from recognition that Being is the only sacred absolute, and bring a serenity that angst-ridden religion fails to provide. I will attempt to show that monotheistic religion contributes greatly to our problem with Otherness. And finally, that sacredness is closely linked to morality and its place in the life of the city.

The following chapters will suggest how the major problems of our era could be affected by a transformation of attitudes toward the sacred based on scientific knowledge. This would take us from a purely intellectual recognition of the systems approach, which forms the basis of evolution and ecology, to a point at which we could satisfy our spiritual needs by modifying our relation to violence, death and Having. The foundation for these ideas was laid by Alan Watts, whose views will be developed in this chapter.

Having come to the conclusion that Western religions had strayed too far from the mysticism that had once characterized all faiths, Watts introduced the non-dualistic religions to a large and mainly youthful audience in California, collecting an impressive following, especially among those opposed to the Vietnam War. Regrettably, the influence of Watts' contemporary, Marcuse, together with the counter-cultural lifestyle of both, delayed wider recognition of the scientific validity of his spiritual quest for several decades. And yet, it provides a bridge between today's sense of loss and our conquests - independence of mind and a taste for pleasure and action - that fall into the trough of an emptiness our common sense denies.

While Marcuse equated pleasure with freedom, Watts related it to mystical delight. However, because of his aversion to what he called the dourness of Christianity, he divorced pleasure from the morality that flows from awareness of Being, leaving us to pick up the pieces. Watts' reflections on spirituality were based on the similarities between the Hindu-Buddhist-Taoist notion of an eternal renewal, and the modern theory of ecosystems. For Taoists, so-called opposites are complementary and Yin/Yang, life and death grow out of each other as part of the same Whole, make Being the only absolute:

> The Tao that can be expressed
> Is not the eternal Tao.
> The Tao is nowhere to be found
> Yet it nourishes and completes all things.
> All things are born from Being
> Being is born from non-Being.

Taoism never gives orders, never admonishes. It simply says what is. When sentient beings know that Being is the only absolute, they do not require orders from an external authority. Half of the Taoist canon, the *Tao Te Ching*, advises rulers to be modest:

> A country is ruled by laws
> A war is made by surprise
> But it's through not-doing
> That the Universe is obtained
> How do I know this?
> By what follows:
>
> The more interdictions and prohibitions
> The poorer the people become.
> The more sharp weapons one has
> The more disorder reigns.
> The more developed imagination
> The more strange products appear.
> The more laws and directives
> The more bandits and thieves.
> That is why the saint says:
> If I practice not-doing
> The people transform themselves
> If I like calm
> The people correct themselves

If I undertake nothing
The people prosper
If I nourish no desires
The people itself returns to simplicity.

The 'Oriental' approach has been seen as fatalism; but when the negatives engendered by the positives are taken into account, agitation does not necessarily produce better results than would a system's spontaneous processes. I believe that highlighting the sense of the sacred that is expressed in every religion would lead to a more meaningful transformation of the human condition than has been achieved by religion. Before Watts, Aldous Huxley had shown that the quest of mystics from every religion was for 'an entity', rather than the God of monotheistic religious traditions, because unlike God, who stands above the Whole it *is* the Whole, of which humans partake, *tat tvam asi* that art thou, 'that' being the Whole.

Aldous Huxley's *The Perennial Philosophy* is a compendium of writings that carries that non-dualist concept forward through the ages.

The 13th century German philosopher and mystic Thomas Eckhart anticipated quantum physics when he wrote: "The knower and the known are one. The more God is in all things, the more he is outside them, the more he is within, the more without."

According to Hillel, a rabbi contemporary of Jesus, Jehovah said: "If I am here, everyone is here. If I am not here, no one is here."

The Taoist Sen T'se: "When ten thousand things are viewed in their oneness, we return to the Origin and remain where we have always been."

The Muslim/Hindu poet and saint, Kabir, sensing the ambiguity in dualism, wrote in the 15th century: "Behold but One in all things; it is the second that leads you astray."

The contemporary Egyptologist Christian Jacq notes that: "Pharaoh is fully conscious that men are attracted by opposites; his role is not to make these eternal realities disappear, but to sublimate them through communion."

The emphasis on state-of-being, in other words, 'is-ness' rather than 'such-ness', (as in *tat tvam asi,* that *art* thou*)*, epitomizes the link between Taoism and modern science. When Huxley says that "the immanent eternal self is one with the Absolute Principle of all existence," he is saying that man is part of the Whole.

Before I go any further with this discussion, I would like to ask the non-scientifically educated reader to take this chapter and those that follow less as a challenge and more as something akin to the 'good news' of the gospel. For me at least, the notions presented here transform science from an intimidating and cold demonstration into a pleasure equal to that of a great symphony or a master painting, and it is this pleasure that can transform struggle against the world into cooperation.

Take David Bohm, for instance, one of the physicists whose work comes close to proving that mind and matter are one. Playfully, he tells us that: "Our thinking follows an ancient Greek mode according to which only Being *is.* Therefore, Non-Being *is not.* This mode of thinking gives us a practical tool for dealing with the world, but it does not describe what happens.

In reality, non-Being also *is*. Both Being and Non-Being are 'that-which-is'. Everything, even 'emptiness', is 'that-which-is'. There is nothing which is not 'that-which-is'. From 'empty space' supposedly there comes something, which disappears again into 'empty space'".

Wow! Not only did we make up the idea of God, we also made up the notion of empty space! In *The Dancing Wu Li Masters,* the amateur handbook on the new physics, Gary Zukav chimes in. "There is no such thing in the world as empty space. All the parts of the universe are connected in an intimate and immediate way." (Zukav's fascination with the new physics ultimately led him to reincarnation. I shall not follow him there.)

Neither Zukav nor Watts have the stature of Huxley, but I agree with Watts' hedonistic view of religion as involving not worship but delight: *Tat tvam asi,* that are thou, and this is cause for delight.

> Christian joy refers to the fact that the Lord is everywhere. The canticle of the three children and Daniel's canticle of the creatures could be taken for Indian, Shintoist or Hindu incantations to nature, and were intended to enable Christians to take part in the rhythm of divine life itself. Every morning at sunrise, Christians are supposed to laugh, clap their hands, kiss, beat drums and electric guitars (sic) to laud God. When the believer sings 'glory to God' he is supposed to perceive the fact that God is rather than that He does.

Alas, the determining factor in Western culture is the notion of an invisible all-powerful Other, separating man from his environment, underlining each man's fear of each other, impeding cognition and autopoiesis, thereby shifting the focus from self-making to making. And with the loss of autopoiesis goes the loss of internal authority, as well as responsibility. In a flash of insight, Boris Cyrulnik muses:

> Thus 'Truth' is the dogma that led humans from freedom to external authority and violence, and revealed truth was probably the concept of one God proclaimed by the world's major religions. Everything was fine until one day someone suggested: 'We are going to submit ourselves to an idea rather than a territory. You go on loving things, we are going to invent a message.' Creative violence, the cauldron of humanity had been born, the marvelous and the horrible had mated to produce civilization.

The same view of the origins of civilization was implied by Freud in his last work, *Moses*. Seeing monotheism as the cause of religious intolerance, he observed that: "With a remarkable intuition of future scientific thought, (Akhenaton) declared solar energy to be the source of all living things, representing justice and truth, and ordered it to be worshipped exclusively, creating the first monotheist religion."

Now this is where the story of Moses gets really interesting: Worship has always served to invoke power, especially power over death. Although the Pharaohs could not defeat death, they organized death to imitate life. Pharaoh's power served first of all to maintain the basis of Egyptian civilization, Ma'at, which embodied the Rule, Justice, and Truth, so that his subjects would enjoy the well-being for which he was responsible. This was the context in which the Pharaoh Akhenaton, who was Moses' contemporary, decreed that Ma'at be represented by the sun, which would replace idols as the unique object of worship.

(The eminent biologist Lynn Margulis evokes Akhenaton in *What is Life?* which she wrote with her son Dorian Sagan. "Ancient religious traditions that considered terrestrial creatures, especially man, to be children of the sun, were far nearer the truth than is thought by those who see earthly beings as simply ephemeral creations arising from the blind and accidental play of matter and forces.")

Akhenaton's insight had to wait until the twentieth century to be recognized by science, but imagine how things might have gone had it been welcomed as confirming the Egyptians' non-dualistic assumption that both men and things were of the same essence, with Western religions following suit! The Italian philosopher monk Giordano Bruno tried to make this happen in the sixteenth century, but he ran afoul of the Inquisition. Margulis and Sagan pay tribute to Bruno for insisting that life comes from the sun:

> Espousing a Pantheistic perspective in which God, life and mind were part of an ever-changing universe, Bruno thought distant worlds might harbor intelligent beings. The same Christian view that Bruno defied holds firm today: God is as superior to the Universe as mind is to matter, or soul is to body. Flesh, a necessary evil, is unclean, only spirit is pure....Bruno blended matter with energy, finite with infinite, world with God.

Unfortunately for us, Akhenaton's successors, pressured by the priests in charge of idols, ordered the Egyptians back to worshiping these latter. In doing so, they paved the way for Moses, then Christ and Mohammad, to place man and God outside of nature, separating God from man, and men from each other. This required a conceptual revolution: Moses' God first defined himself as the non-dualistic 'He who is', not very different, after all, from 'the invisible' to which the Egyptians referred when they thought of God anthropomorphically. However, since 'He who is' was two conceptual steps beyond idols (though invisible, God was a being in the image of man), the message had to be simplified in order to be widely understood. The non-dualistic 'He who is' was sacrificed to the dualistic idea that it was better to worship He who had power over the Whole, than the Whole itself.

With the invention of God, transcendence superseded immanence and the notion of Otherness with a capital O was born. God was not only 'Other', as were idols, He, rather than a mortal Pharaoh, was the Supreme Other, and it was his ability to dominate nature that made him so. (Although Pharaoh was the most powerful among men, he needed the Gods to dominate nature.)

When Moses created the Deity in the image of man, he emphasized His power, rather than the overarching principle of life for which sacredness stands. Men must know that they were fundamentally different from other animate beings, and follow the One who, though made in their image, was the epitome of Otherness, since he possessed powers unavailable to them. It would have been difficult for worship of either the sun, or idols that were half-man half beast, to lead to the notion of supreme Otherness that we associate with God.

Another difference between the Sun and an invisible God is that although men see themselves as created in His image, God like man, spoke, and thus, gave orders. Very differently, Akhenaton's sun was content to be, since it represented an idea, and it was Pharaoh who, to ensure respect of the idea, gave orders.

We may assume that Truth, Cyrulnik's 'horrible' component in civilization, originated with Moses' reinterpretation of the notion of Supreme Other formulated by Akhenaton. When he declared that the divine entity was neither the sun nor any idol, but an invisible being in whose image men had been created, Moses changed men's relation to the universe. Some of his followers were tempted to continue worshipping idols, but no command could have bent the others *because they recognized God's power over them.*

The religion of ancient Egypt, structured around the relationship of man to the Cosmos, is often confused with Greco-Roman mythology, but unlike myth, with its emphasis on power, it did not become part of the Western heritage. And yet, like Taoists, who emphasize the unknowableness of reality, the Egyptians drew behavioral precepts from their perception of the oneness of the Universe, while the Judeo-Christian world began by analyzing God, debating for centuries whether He was immanent or transcendent, whether He was His own cause, what this meant for free will, and whether He could know or do this or that. In so doing, it removed God from the human world of representation, separating itself from Cyrulnik's 'context', the immediacy of the Gods, who are one with Nature, and turning to signs. Instead of rituals based on instinctive knowledge of man's oneness with Nature, such as those practiced by the Egyptians, the Judeo-Christian world transformed Yin/Yang into tit for tat.

The reason for that is as follows: if God's supreme power makes Him the epitome of Otherness, then human Others also have potential power over us, and must be feared. Remember Capra's definition of autopoiesis as a network pattern in which the function of each component is to participate in the production or transformation of other components. As opposed to that 'self-making', 'making' involves the creation of defenses between each individual and each other. And unlike God, human Others who stand in the way of making can be overcome with the hatred born of fear. Neighbors are the most proximate others, and potentially as threatening as a distant enemy. How different is that notion from Egyptian morality, in which each individual was responsible for the preservation of each other, through constant observance of Ma'at!

Until they started to worship a Supreme Other, what had counted most for Hebrews and Egyptians alike was existing, not their differences. With the notion of difference came the desire to exist in certain ways. And those who did not conform were dealt with. As Cyrulnik notes: "'My God is better (i.e., more powerful) than yours', soon became: 'My God is the only true God. That is the truth, and in all justice, I must kill you if you refuse to believe it.'"

At the end of the day, a culture represents first and foremost that to which it answers, whether it be a person or an idea. The West's representation of human Others passes through the prism of our representation of God, and our degree of internal authority is in inverse proportion to our perceived obligation to answer to Him. (The more direct the link between a ruler and God, the more absolute the former's power. Louis the XIVth was merely a ruler by divine right, compared to Akhenaton, who was the earthly incarnation of the

Sun.) Nationalism too can be all the better defended that it is linked to religion (God and country, Gott mit uns, In God We Trust...). That is why, embodied in the notion of sovereignty as well as in religion, Otherness has become a permanent cause of violence.

As Watts wrote thirty years ago in his flippant but highly effective style: "The radical disjunction between Creation and Creator constitutes the major specificity of the three great modern monotheistic religions. Securely ensconced in ancient history, or elsewhere in some improbable paradise, Christ can no longer be the beggar who knocks at the door."

Underlining the absurdity of dualism, which flows from the Otherness of God, he asks:

> If I am forbidden to even think that I can experience complete union with God and fraternally share his meal, how can I believe I can see Him in the face of my boorish neighbor? If, by following Christ's path I cannot become divine, why should I follow him? Not everyone can be the boss's son and be allowed to chat with God the Father. And if I cannot see in my boorish neighbor's eye even the palest reflection of God and my own soul, how could I see it in my dog, the heron flying overhead, the nervures of an oak or the sparkle of a fragment of granite mica?

Watts saw all ideologies, including atheism, as a form of idolatry. He proposed a new type of ecumenism, which would have been a dialogue rather than an ideology. Unfortunately, he was scarcely heard above the din of the Cold War, with its accompanying belief that everything would be all right if only our standoff with the Soviet Union could end without blowing up the planet. The Cold War ended with little more than a whimper, as processes (as opposed to acts), are wont, and precisely because it went unrecognized as a process composed of many elements, the world did not come together, but continued to unravel, this time in the name of religion.

The reader may ask how it is that Hindus, who do not believe in one God, are capable of the most horrific atrocities against Muslims. The answer, I think is that- Britain's centuries long colonization of India, followed by the reign of films, radio and television, brought about a linear us-them mindset.

And yet, Unicity which has been around since men began reflecting on the nature of the universe and their place in it, is much closer to the modern ethos than the idea of God upon which the monotheistic religions are based. When we call upon God, we are wishing for certainty - a closed system, in which, however, things would continue instead of inevitably running down. Whether we see God as part of our system, fixing everything, or of another system that provides energy and takes in waste, we assume a hierarchical relationship rather than integration. This dualism propels us toward more separation, domination and instabilities, creating ever more totalitarian and less symbiotic systems.

Often humans invent a personalized God as an alibi for their inability to overcome disorder. 'It's God's will, not mine', or, 'I'm only obeying Him' (rejecting responsibility). 'Suffering doesn't matter, as long as God loves you," or 'Open your mind to my word' (and everything will be all right). In its search for order, the Judeo-Greco tradition created closed systems, which citizens then try to open, while for the Egyptians, Ma'at represented a need to simply tend toward order in an open system subject to both order and disorder.

The repulsion many intellectuals feel for religion prevents them from imagining that there may be an alternative to revealed truth other than irrational sects. Yet the American Indians pray to 'he who is invisible and eternal', and consider singing as the breathing of the spirit which consecrates the act of living. And according to Watts, when Christ in the Eucharist says that: 'this is my body' he intended the same thing as the Hindu 'that art thou';

> When he invented Mass, Christ was not seeking to commemorate a specific historic event, but to initiate a permanent celebration of the redemption of the material universe, which we now see as a prison.

The fact that all religions constitute an amalgam of beautiful ideas and absurd beliefs (generally added in a second period), and that clergymen often serve more political than spiritual goals (including their own), confirms the reasoned atheism or agnosticism of most intellectuals, including this writer. Another reason why we flee religion is because we associate it with death: although unable to protect us from it, God is linked to the religious rituals that surround it. Atheists affirm in essence that humans do not need a God to accept death. I am suggesting that God is simply another word for order/disorder. How else to explain that 'He' is both good and evil, that He has created a wondrous world for us to enjoy - and ethnic cleansing? That He seems to reward crime while heaping scorn upon the righteous?

Watts was highly irritated by what he called "uncompromising, militant, rigorous, authoritarian and totally sanctimonious Christianity, whose fanatic insistence on the absolute separation between creatures and the Creator endangers the survival of the species." Thirty years after his death, Christian institutions look quite different, but their basic premise, that God is outside and above the world of man leaves unresolved the problem of Otherness, Violence and Having.

Where does all this leave us with respect to the subject of this book, the possibility of 'a Taoist politics'?Although power over the order/disorder dyad is an illusion, as are the rewards of prayer, the new sciences suggest that we can use cognition to transform closed political systems into open systems in order to better manage our relations with others. As a bonus, when we recognize the crucial role of internal authority, we would be able to accept a constant state of order/ disorder relieved by phase transitions.

The notion of a steady state has been misinterpreted in the public mind as 'static'. Actually, a 'steady state' is a magic moment in the vibrant regime of order/ disorder, poised, far from equilibrium, at the edge of chaos, where cognition and autopoiesis take place. The biologist Stuart Kauffman believes that "only God has the wisdom to understand the final law, the throws of the quantum dice," however, his research appears to show that there is no final law. I believe that when we realize that there is nothing we must believe in, we recover our internal authority. Knowing that the world simply 'is' and that we are part of it, should help us realize that authority resides in our-selves, as an intrinsic part of the Whole. And this suggests the possibility of a new sense of sacredness that is neither an opiate, a mystery, nor, to use Watt's favorite word, dour, but is consistent with an open political system?

Although Watts enjoyed his status as guru, he maintained that each individual had to find his own way, and that praying, whether kneeling or in the lotus position, was not what religion was about. Religion was simply the recognition that God - the Tao, the Buddha, the Atman - was everywhere, yet undefinable. Reason requires definitions, but to define is to separate. The religious ceremonies and prayers practiced by the major religions are very similar, and our institutional Gods - every one of them - are the epitome of Otherness.

A new spirituality based on the notion of Unicity can lead each person wherever he chooses, allowing believers to recognize that all religions are founded on the same basic mysticism, and non-believers to find de-light - and therefore serenity - in the existence of an all-embracing Cosmos that requires neither guru nor trim-mings. The notion of Unicity should help us move away from that of a Supreme Other incarnated in God, and thus from our inherent fear of all Others. The fact that the Universal Mind is the inner consciousness of 'he who is' (Buddha, God, the Atman, the Unnamable or whatever one wishes to call 'Is- ness'), makes each of us with our consciousness a part of It, and each Other a part of Ourselves.

Neither prison nor dictatorship can take away our internal freedom, that is our thoughts and beliefs, be-cause they are part of the consciousness, cognition and autopoiesis that constitute the essence of Man and the Cosmos. Unlike consciousness, through which each individual partakes of the Whole that includes each Other, 'conscience' differentiates one individual from another. When conscience is part of all-embracing con-sciousness, Otherness is no longer an absolute. When it is not, it leads a life of its own, ever further removed from the Whole.

It is remarkable that although freedom of conscience forms the basis of the secular state, the separation of church and state in no way prevents men from hating each other because they see God differently. It is because we see religion as being 'out there', rather than within ourselves, that we think beliefs can be curtailed - thus allowing them to become a *casus belli*. And it is because religion - unlike spirituality - requires the accomplish-ment of rites, i.e., actions, that men are not content with merely being free to believe.

When soldiers are fortified by a religious idea, they feel invincible, thus even when we view strife as unreasonable, we cannot eliminate it. Unicity can serve to diffuse conflict, because the fact that each individual is consciousness, and therefore linked to the Whole, is a stronger idea than the fact that each individual has two eyes and warm blood. When God (the Buddha, Shiva, the Atman), is in each of us, we need fear nor hate any Other. When Otherness is attenuated, our external freedom no longer runs up against the freedom of the Other, because each of us is grounded, or reassured, in the knowledge that she is part of an infinite Whole. My internal freedom is my ground, your internal freedom is your ground, and we both sit as lilies on a pond.

And when we no longer expect to find absolutes, when we know there are no definitive solutions, we can begin to practice what many are calling for: A politics of love and compassion, meaning one of morality, which we shall now consider through two prisms: the relative and the absolute.

X
The Sacred, the Absolute and the Relative

That which is is that which is. There is
nothing which is not that which is. There
is nothing other than that which is. We are
part of that which is. In fact, we are that which is.
Gary Zukav

After a lengthy period during which Western philosophy seemed preoccupied mainly with science and
politics, both of which emphasize linear analysis of
'facts', morality is slowly coming to the fore. However,
it continues to be based upon the authority of God,
which is perhaps why it has failed to make giant strides.

There appear to have been two basic interpretations of morality in the Christian world: the Protestant
and the Catholic. The former defines ethics as "a principle of right or good conduct, concerned with judging
the goodness or evil of human action and character.
Arising from conscience, or the sense of right and
wrong: a moral obligation." The Roman Catholic definition is less subjective: "The science of good and evil,
a theory of human action as subjected to duty and having as its purpose the good." Both definitions, inspired
by the absolute authority of God that derives from his
Otherness, imply that principles are absolute, while
paradoxically submitting them to judgement.

It was clear thousands of years ago, and still
should be today, that morality follows not from 'princi-

ples', but from the imperative of preserving Being. The Ten Commandments condemn actions that could ultimately threaten life. 'Thou shalt not kill' is an imperative that transcends all else, because Being is an absolute that can be subject neither to discussion nor judgement. Sacredness, on the other hand, is defined as 'belonging to a separate, inviolable domain; worthy of absolute respect, an absolute value'. From the moment something becomes a value, it is open to discussion (as in the North/South disagreement over values). But by allowing values to justify horrific crimes, the West adjectivizes - or categorizes - Being, destroying the notion that it is sacred and absolute. Western culture calls God sacred and sees this as a value. But God represents power rather than Being, hence when we worship God we are valuing power. Displacing immanence, the notion that God is *of* the universe, transcendence, his absolute power *over* it, has led to unbridled violence - and despair.

It is because Eastern cultures privilege immanence that they regard Being as sacred. This notion was elaborated in two ancient historical periods in different parts of the world. The first was about halfway between the second and first millennium B.C.E., the second about a millennium later. In the first period, Hinduism appeared in India, while Bronze Age civilization in Greece turned the Mediterranean world toward rationalization. In the second period, Gautama Buddha lived in India, Lao Tzu and Confucius wrote in China, and Athens completed its quest for rationality.

In the Eastern civilizations, men knew that the meaning of life is intimately involved with morality, and autopoiesis confirms that authority is an inherent quality from which morality derives. Morality, in turn, implies an obligation to preserve the Whole of which we are a part. **When we seek a deity outside ourselves, we place the meaning of life outside ourselves, renouncing our inner authority and giving external authority absolute power over the Whole.**

It is unfortunate that many people who reject the authority of God, still fail to understand that morality is about responsibility rather than obedience. Freedom of conscience led to the Enlightenment, whose embrace of rationality excised the morality linked to religion from the body politic. Having thrown the baby of immanence and responsibility out with the bathwater of blind faith, modernity made transcendence - and power - the bedrock of Western civilization.

In the linear context that flows from God as a transcendent entity, responsibility is of the If......then type. In a circular context, in which God is immanent, responsibility flows from awareness that opposites are complementary, each being inseparable from the Whole. When good and bad are seen as following each other in a continuous counter-balancing rather than pulling in opposite directions, it becomes clear that circumstances are best evaluated by each individual's internal authority rather than by the rigidity of external authority. Linear Western societies recognize this when they entrust decisions about capital punishment to juries rather than an individual judge reading from a codebook.

However, in matters of life and death, i.e., respecting or not respecting Being as the only absolute, evaluation of 'right' and 'wrong' should not be the only factor. There is a difference between evaluations that can freely be translated into acts and those that should not be. This notion is best illustrated by the disputes over abortion and capital punishment. Pro-life/pro-capital punishment advocates rightly define life as sacred, however their if.....then, linear reasoning implies that all judgements can be freely translated into acts. They consider that if a person has committed murder, he deserves to die, while an unborn fetus, having harmed no one, must not be prevented from reaching a viable state. This blurs the fact that although the right to judge, or hold an opinion, is part of our internal, absolute freedom, because we can only strive toward truth, judgement cannot justify killing.

Pro-abortionists and opponents of capital punishment are unable to argue convincingly why their respective positions are justified because they are not familiar with the new biology's implications for morality. The science of complexity provides compelling evidence that life had to occur, given the marvelous self-organizational capabilities of the biological process. Referring again to Stuart Kauffman:

> When the number of different kinds of molecules in a chemical soup passes a certain threshold, a self-sustaining network of reactions will suddenly appear. Not because of a mysterious élan vital, but thanks to the simple, profound transformation of dead molecules into an organization by which each molecule's formation is catalyzed by some other molecule in the organization. Given a supply of 'food' molecules, the network will be able to recreate itself indefinitely. Like the metabolic networks that inhabit every living cell, it will be alive.(...) Life, at its root, lies in the property of catalytic closure among a collection of molecular species. Alone, each molecular species is dead. Jointly, once

catalytic closure is achieved, the collective system of molecules is alive.

To clarify: Molecule A and molecule B, when left alone, will eventually catalyze to form molecule C. However, if A and B find themselves in the presence of D, which acts as a catalyzer, then they will form molecule C much faster. In turn, A, B, and C may catalyze other reactions. This is known as a collectively auto catalytic system, in which molecules speed up the very reactions by which they themselves are formed: A makes B; B makes C; C makes A again, and this process illustrates Being-as-part-of-the-Whole.

If we consider merely the fact that Being is sacred, then abortion and capital punishment are both murder. But the processes that make life inevitable also suggest that the existence of any particular, specific life is fraught with uncertainties, and this should change the debate over abortion.. Arguments center on the question of when life begins, and while a human life begins with fertilization, as in collective catalytic closure, the prior meeting and mating of two people is an eminently random event. Following this, nature's own caprices can affect the potential of a resulting fetus to develop into a viable human being; and just as truly, external factors beyond the mother's control can condemn a child to adverse life conditions.

If we consider that humans are part of nature, we must accept that human evaluations of the appropriateness of allowing fetal development are no more absolutely 'right' or 'wrong' than nature's partly random processes. They are responsible if they proceed from a sincere assessment of known factors that are likely to affect the fetus' future outside the womb. A woman's choice is not a question of rights, but of recognizing the limits of human control over events, and of making good faith decisions. There is no reason to reject a decision that affects an organism's survival because it is taken by a 'human' instead of being a 'fact of nature', since both humans and nature are part of the Whole.

Alas, with our dualistic heritage, in which right and wrong, like good and bad, are absolutes, no 'right' can be infringed. Desirable limitations on First or Second Amendment rights bring the same fear of a slippery slope as the issue of women's rights. But external freedom, i.e., freedom to act, is no more an absolute for humans than it is for the rest of the natural world.

A woman should have exclusive jurisdiction over her body, through which she exists, without coming under the authority of spouses, doctors or clergy. But by the same token, the existence of a fetus, which is unable to make decisions, is synonymous with *its* body. During the first six or seven months of pregnancy, the body of a fetus is only potentially that of a human being capable of life outside the womb, hence the mother's right to dispose of her body can be opposed to the fetus's potential right to its body. However, the mother's external freedom ends where the potential freedom of a viable fetus begins.

When the right of a woman to make decisions about her body favors her quality of life or short-term comfort over a responsible evaluation of a viable fetus's chances of living a reasonably satisfying life through adoption, we cross an ethical line. Fear on the part of pro-choicers that a total ban on a rarely needed type of abortion may at some future date jeopardize basic abortion rights also trumps responsibility. The debate over late-term or 'partial birth' abortion shows that both sides of the right-to-life/pro-choice debate may be placing rights above sacredness. As in every instance where 'rationalism' wins out over wisdom, too much of a good thing can result in horror.

Women usually know within the first months of pregnancy whether they should be able to ensure a reasonable existence to their offspring. If for any reason, a negative conclusion is reached later, the woman's responsibility is to bring the child to term if it can be expected to lead a healthful life through adoption. The fact that in all cultures, at all times, early abortion has been practiced with relative equanimity, while the killing of babies by marauding soldiers evokes horror, should alert us to the fact that in this debate we have lost sight of basic morality. There are relatively few cases in which the life of a woman in her third term of pregnancy is in greater danger from delivery than from an abortion, or in which it is discovered that a fetus is not viable. It should be possible to craft legislation that allows those pregnancies to be interrupted without opening the door to abuse.

Turning now to capital punishment, the existence of that which is sacred - Being - cannot be contingent upon actions resulting from judgement or opinion. Although we are free to judge an individual, we are not entitled to transform that judgement, or opinion - or even certainty - into an act which terminates Being, unless we can affirm that judgement, and therefore thought processes, are infallible. Every life is subject to accidents or illness, including that of a murderer, who may die a natural or accidental death. The magistrate or jury are thus on an equal footing with a drunken driver or a virus, their 'sentences' no more certainly 'right' than the interactions between molecules, or those of egg and sperm.

When we are talking about the probable future life conditions of a fetus once it becomes an infant, we are not judging Being, we are evaluating future circumstances, which are by definition beyond our control. We can act on this evaluation, aware that we may be mistaken. When capital punishment is applied, death is not contingent upon circumstances beyond our control, but upon judgement, which can be fallible. When we inflict capital punishment, we are transforming our freedom to think, which is total, into freedom to act, which is not.

Both sides in the debate need to link the notion of responsibility to Being, realizing that the competition between religion and government for power over men does not make morality any less crucial to life.

In *Human Rights as Idolatry and Politics* Michael Ignatieff properly notes that human rights are indispensable to protect individuals against unjust laws and orders. But since justice is the application of evaluations and judgements to the ever changing process of Being, it can only be subjective and relative. And unlike a belief in God or the notion of Truth, belief in the sacredness of life leads to recognition of both individual internal authority, and the need for justice in the exercise of external authority.

It's because sacredness is about Being that justice is above humanity. Calling justice divine does not imply that it comes from God, but that it is independent of intrinsic human qualities or defects. The imperative of tending toward justice does not imply that it is an absolute. Rather, we must defend justice because failure to do so disrespects the sacredness of life. We must tend toward it, even though men are dishonest, cowardly, self-serving, and do not individually and at all times deserve that we care about them. When we understand that justice is not to be defended because people deserve it, but because it defends life, it becomes clear that all men are entitled to it.

Like many contemporary scientists, Kauffman sees a need for sacredness: "I hold the hope that the new sciences of complexity may help us find anew our place in the universe, that through this new science, we may recover our sense of worth, our sense of the sacred." Kauffman tells us that "life - complex, whole, emergent - is a natural out-growth of the world in which we live". Thus, Being is sacred because the world unalterably 'is'. Giordano Bruno expressed the same conviction:

> Everything that makes diversity of kinds, species, differences, properties, everything which depends on generation, corruption, alienation and change is not being or existence, but is a condition and circumstance of being or existence which is one, infinite, immobile, subject, matter, life, soul, truth and good.

Modern biology - and as we shall presently see, physics - is extremely useful in confronting human issues as well as the planetary crisis. Biologists today recognize that evolution involves interactions between Darwinian chance and selection, and self-organization, or "auto catalytic closure acting on non-equilibrium systems". As Kauffman explains: "Life is a natural expression of a universe that is not in equilibrium, evolving toward a regime that is poised between order and chaos."

What religious dogma can compete with that for thrills?

If we could accept that 'life in its abundance was bound to arise, not as a highly improbable accident, but as an expected fulfillment of the natural order,' we could lessen our existential angst and increase our ability to deal with chaos, knowing, as Kauffman tells us, that: "We truly are at home in the universe". Secure in our place, we would have less reason to abridge other lives on the basis of subjective judgement, to insist on 'purifying' other peoples or positing rights as absolutes.

Accepting that order arises from chaos, instead of pushing ever forward toward the chimerical goal of achieving absolute order, we could take our cue from ancient Egypt, whose geography made it singularly aware of the relationship between man and the cosmos. Like Orientals, the ancient Egyptians knew what we must now rediscover: that morality is intimately linked to Being. We shall refer to Taoism in a moment, for now let us return to ancient Egypt, whose essence has been largely overlooked by the general public in favor of its bizarre accouterments.

The Egyptian world view can be likened to an open system, its mixture of free will and predestination the subject of an elegant feedback loop. In the previous chapter, we saw that it was Ma'at, the notion of order, or the just measure of things, that underlay the world and commanded men's actions. Ma'at had come to man from the gods at the moment of creation, and was constantly returned to them through his intermediary, that is, his on-going collaboration and response to them. Creation was the work of a divine hand, however it consisted in a process of constant transformation (as with the molecules in a chemical soup). The order of Ma'at had always been challenged by disorder, even before the Gods came on the scene, but according to the Egyptologist Erik Hornung: "The daily offering of bread, beer and incense to Ma'at by the Pharaoh showed that the human sphere, with all the fragile, uncertain connections upon which it depended, was an open system, a far-from-equilibrium steady state, as it was at the moment of creation."

Rather than material gifts, the Gods needed a human response - or feedback - to their existence. For their 'creative opus' to have lasting meaning, men had to bear witness in their hearts to its existence. Silence, the absence of response, implied non-existence, while the world of existence was an on-going dialogue between the Gods and man.

How far they were from transcendence, those ancient Egyptians! It was not power for power's sake that was sacred, but power in the service of Being. As Freud noted: "Akhenaton was proud to enjoy the creation of his own life in Ma'at." Even after a particularly bloody war, the Egyptians did not say 'never again', because they knew that battle, confrontation, confusion and a questioning of the established order were necessary characteristics of the world of existence. Evil was already inherent in the nonexistent, thus there was no need to fault the Gods when injustice occurred; they were doing their best. However, since Ma'at was forever being troubled, a constant effort on the part of the Gods and men was required to prevent disorder from reaching a point where it endangered justice and well-being. In modern terms, before runaway energy reached a bifurcation point!

As Hornung writes: "By requiring the Gods and men to limit disorder, creation made them jointly responsible for preserving existence, while realizing that limited disorder was indispensable to a living order." Egyptian society remained immobile - or just far enough from equilibrium - for so long that it managed to guard against bifurcations, which could as well lead to positive change as to disaster.

The felicitous situation of ancient Egypt - an abundance of the goods of life and a homogeneous community - exists in only a few places today. But it was thanks to beliefs that were consonant with what we call sustainable development, that Egyptians were able to preserve their civilization over three thousand years. The Nile, which constantly renewed the soil, provided the conditions for an ecological way of life, and the Egyptians knew that it was their responsibility to preserve it. This meant participating in the immense building projects Pharaoh initiated to honor the gods, since he was responsible for obtaining from them the people's well-being. (Egypt was less successful from the moment her neighbors ventured across her borders, precisely because, as Aries would say, it had for so long lacked upheavals.)

And yet, partly thanks to its desert-bound isolation from other civilizations, Egypt experienced a peaceful continuity for over three thousand years, while the Roman Empire' lasted only three hundred or so and Hitler's Reich twelve. While Egypt experienced the serenity of a secure, protected place for each person, the Roman Empire signaled man's loss of place. As Hans Jonas has noted: "The autonomous, self-governing cities lost their foundations, becoming mere administrative entities," as men became for the first time citizens of what could only be for them an abstract empire, its seat far removed from their lands.

Power, rather than sacredness, was the foundation of that empire, and, like the Greek example, it was accompanied by a basic disregard for Being. (The Greeks played, according to the rules of the Gods, but the Romans meant business, according to the laws of man.) In a country that viewed murder as a logical component of conquest and power, the orphan and the widow were protected, however the penalty for insulting the State was death, and early Christians, who affirmed that killing was a sin, had to go underground.

At present we have lost not only our place, but the security upon which serenity is based. Polemics over abortion and capital punishment, ethnic purification and human rights wrack our anxiety-ridden society. But they represent merely the visible angst of a civilization that separated Being from that which gave it meaning - its essence as part of the Whole - and thus never really granted the individual human life its rightful place. Among pro-lifers the defense of life is not a defense of Being as a concept, but as a right that justifies action. Yet, when science reconstructs life's inevitability, it is Eastern and Egyptian circular thought that it upholds, rather than the Western or linear canon upon which our laws are based.

Egyptian civilization is considered the forerunner of our own, yet we view the ancient Egyptians as a highly conservative people obsessed with death, rather than realizing that, considering themselves blessed by the Gods, they so enjoyed life that they wanted its pleasures to continue in an afterlife. I am proposing that we give pride of place to that interpretation, for it can help provide us with a sound basis for ecological morality. Once we know that life arises from chaos, we should be able to accept the need to constantly strive toward order by cooperating with 'the Gods', instead of pitting ourselves against nature until it returns the abuse. Both nature and society require not external authority but the sense of responsibility that flows from awareness of the Whole .

A Tao-like - or Egyptian - sense of responsibility, recognizes that Being, the autopoietic Yin/Yang, is the only Absolute. The formal gap between Taoism and ancient Egyptian culture, one being relatively anarchistic and the other highly structured, suggests that the point is not to return to religions or philosophies of the past, but to a basic spirit they share. An appropriate notion would be that Western civilization has spun out of orbit with respect to the circle that represents Unicity, and that a fundamental change in our world view could help it return. As the Tao Te Ching says: "To be big is to stretch out. To stretch out implies going far. Being far requires a return". Western civilization is big, and stretches out, but if it does not return to the notion of Being as the sole absolute, it will over-shoot and crash.

Now, as always, the masses need rituals and communion, while intellectuals require their serenity to be based on logic. By adding a touch of poetic intuition to scientific certainties, Taoism can bring serenity to non-believers while softening the impact of Otherness on believers. And by defining morality according to Being, the Egyptian notion of Ma'at can inspire both to adopt public and private behaviors likely to foster the sustainable development required for human life on earth to continue.

Having examined here the relationship between morality and sacredness, we shall now turn to that between morality and Otherness, via Buddhism and Taoism. That will lead us to quantum physics, and thence to the effects a spiritual transformation could have on the problems of sustainable development and unemployment.

XI
Otherness, Relativity and Order/Disorder

We are included in the word. It is not
the soul which is in the body, but the
body which is in the soul. And the soul
is that which constitutes the environment,
the entire network of relations and processes
outside of which we are nothing.
Alan Watts

We can assume that in ancient Egypt, the problem of Otherness was seen as part of the natural tendency toward disorder, which morality, through observance of Ma'at, maintained within tolerable limits. Within the dualistic Judeo-Christian or Islamic context, Otherness is not part of a natural disorder requiring constant attention through morality, but part of a disorder that only-God can control.

Like the ancient Egyptian religion, in which disorder flows non-judgementally from existence, Buddhism is based on elaborate intellectual constructs, however unlike Egyptian religion, it considers that everything that happens to humans is a direct consequence of past acts which may even have taken place in previous lives, according to the theory known as the chain of interdependent causes. Although like Taoism and Hinduism, Buddhism has a circular context, it proposes a linear, if...then morality: To avoid suffering in the future, we must behave better in the present!

For Buddhism, our problem with Otherness stems from ignorance, i.e., the illusion of a tangible Self, which inevitably runs up against other Selves. It defines altruism as a moral obligation to diminish the suffering of others, and maintains that until we rid ourselves of our desires, and are thus able to do this, we shall continue to be reborn to a life that can only consist of suffering, with death as the ultimate suffering. Buddhism emphasizes not so much change, which is fluid, as rigidity: we are attached to the wheel of rebirth, or transmigration until, having succeeded in replacing our illusory desires with moral perfection, nirvana delivers us.

Buddhism is centered around the idea that the Self which suffers is an illusion, since we cannot locate it, while in a crucial distinction, Taoism emphasizes the notion of an unnameable Whole. It sees no problem with Otherness, has no immanent laws or punishment and knows no absolute other than Being. Life is neither all suffering until we are delivered, nor all fun if only we try hard enough. It is an ever changing state, and morality - or ethics - is a path that enables us to live in harmony with the Whole by respecting Being. Its attitude toward immortality is more a striving than a rigidly codified destiny. Death is only mourned when it comes before its time, but Taoism refuses to accommodate killing:

> Arms are evil instruments, repugnant to all. They are not the instruments of a gentleman, who uses them only when forced. For the gentleman honors peace and tranquility, and does not rejoice in victory. Human massacres should be mourned, victory in battle is celebrated with funeral rites.

It is because Western ethics does not condemn war from a spiritual point of view (the sacredness of Being), but from that of morality, with its rationalizations and judgements, that it allows 'just' wars. War is the epitome of linear, if......then, tit for tat thinking, but when order is seen as a circular phenomenon arising from chaos, and Being arises from Non-Being, it becomes almost impossible.

The life of the city includes joys and frustrations, just as individual lives include pleasure and pain. It is fair that we should endeavor to maximize pleasure and minimize suffering, and when we recognize morality's relationship to Being, seeking to diminish the suffering of others becomes an obligation. When we affirm that morality must be based on the recognition that Being is the only Absolute, and that this conviction should form the basis of society, and therefore of politics, we are taking our cue from Taoism and ancient Egypt, rather than from Buddhism, Islam, or the Judeo-Christian ethic. With its basis in causality, Buddhism, like the religions of the book, seems to have by-passed a more fruitful intuition: if events do not have a linear cause, how could suffering have an if......then context?

Paradoxically, Buddhism's current revival in the West is partly due to the new physics, which de-emphasizes linear causality. The new physics lends itself to a variety of psychological and philosophical interpretations, and Buddhists stress those aspects which are remindful of its tradition, while ignoring the fact that they contradict causality. I suspect that one of the reasons for Buddhism's current vogue is the fact that it helps us to become detached from stress-provoking situations. But Taoism, which has no official representative and no organization, suggests a path likely to limit stress-causing situations.

Basing morality on the imperative of responsibility toward the Other and toward the universe upon which our existence depends does not require linear thinking, but recognition of the scientific confirmation of is-ness. Referring to Heisenberg's uncertainty principle, Kauffman notes that although scientists cannot both explain in detail and predict a given phenomenon, they can still have every hope of predicting 'kinds of things'. From my layman's point of view, several 'kinds of political things' might flow from contemporary science.

The interdisciplinary search for emergent order tells us that there appears to be no First Cause, echoing a Taoist intuition. And the new physics and the new biology confirm the Egyptian belief that order and disorder are not distinct entities but constitute the Whole. The theory of relativity implies that there is no such thing as a separate space, independent but empty. It also establishes that appearances are misleading: motion is relative to the position of the observer, space and time are one, and mass is a form of energy. As Gary Zukav tells us: "Quantum theory has proved everything from sub-atomic particles to transistors to stellar energy. It has never failed. It has no competition."

According to Zukav, the matter/energy dichotomy that determines our world view goes back at least as far as the Old Testament:

> Genesis portrays man as a sort of ceramic creation. God scoops up a handful of clay (matter) and breathes life into it (energy).... "The Old Testament is a product of the Western world (or the other way around). Physics is a product of the Western world." Yet paradoxically, the New Physics brings the West-

ern world back to the Eastern world, "where there has never been much philosophical or religious confusion about matter and energy. The world of matter is an illusory world, in that we do not see it as it really is. The way it really is cannot be communicated verbally, however each moment of enlightenment reveals that everything, all the separate parts of the Universe, are manifestations of the same Whole. There is only one reality and it is whole and unified.This is strikingly similar to the picture of physical reality emerging from high-energy particle physics.

For Kauffman, we are "in ways we do not yet see, natural expressions of matter and energy coupled together in non-equilibrium systems". And according to David Bohm:

(Neither) ultimate perception (nor) the subtle mechanism of knowing the truth originates in the brain or in any material structure, although a material structure is necessary to manifest it. (...) Our thought process, based on symbols, imposes upon us the categories of either/or. It confronts us with either this or that, or a mixture of this and that. But in the realm of experience, nothing is either this or that. There is always at least one more alternative, and often an unlimited number of them.

For David Finkelstein:

There are no waves in the game. The equation that the game obeys is a wave equation, but there are no waves running around. There are no particles running around either. What's running around are quanta, the third alternative."

Humans have always wanted to understand the universe, and although we never bargained for quantum theory and its implications, creation legends formulated in different cultures describe its origins in ways hardly less credible than the findings of modern physics. Today, synchronicity is the theory that perhaps comes closest to the spirit of myths and legends. It is defined as the simultaneous existence of two events which do not have a common cause, but have meaning for the person who experiences them. The psychiatrist C.G. Jung and the physicist Wolfgang Pauli, a close friend of Heisenberg, formulated this concept in the nineteen-thirties. The idea of supra-luminal communication (that is, faster than the speed of light, and therefore theoretically impossible), enables quantum mechanics to posit that the universe does not have separate parts, and provides a basis for understanding synchronicity.

F. David Peat's 1987 *Synchronicity* makes the thory accessible to a general readership. Essential to the notions it presents is David Bohm's implicate and explicate order, which Peat explains as a process of continuous enfolding and unfolding.

> The everyday world of solid bodies that are unambiguously located in space and of consequence in a linear time, correspond to what could be called the explicate or unfolded order, which can now be seen as a manifestation of an unfolding from the deeper implicate order....In quantum mechanics, an elementary particle is taken to be the manifestation of an underlying quantum field, and represents the folding of the field into a localized region. The annihilation of the particle is the unfolding back into the field. Thus the complex reactions of elementary particles can be thought of as enfoldings and unfoldings within a dynamic background.

Evoking the work of Varela and Maturana, Peat shows how information creates "a series of interlocking levels of meaning and electro-chemical processes", suggesting that "mind and matter are two orders, or parts, of a single spectrum, which is itself neither matter nor mind, these orders being located at each of its ends as human thresholds, with a whole range of hidden possibilities in between and even beyond."

Peat posits that meaning is the kernel of both material structures and the collective unconscious. "It is at the heart of 'objective intelligence', that formative, generative principle that is neither matter nor mind". The processes of matter and the activity of information are two sides of one reality. Again, according to Peat: "Enfolded within any region of space or particle of matter would be information that potentially applies to the whole universe. Bohm suggests that this implicate order, with its enfolding and unfolding, is characteristic of all reality."

There is a reference to something like enfolding and unfolding in the *Lurianic Kabbalah*. According to Karen Armstrong "creation begins with an act of voluntary exile. The infinite and inaccessible Godhead....had to shrink into itself, evacuating as it were, a region within itself in order to make room for the world." And Stephen Hawking tells us that: "A primordial black hole with an initial mass of a thousand million tons would have a life-time roughly equal to the age of the universe. Primordial black holes with initial masses less than this figure would already have completely evaporated."

As noted in Chapter II, James Lovelock argues convincingly with the Gaia theory that living entities are not just sitting on an inanimate planet, but are the result of the planet's chemical and dynamic processes interacting with the biosphere. Over thousands of millennia, starting with the Big Bang, via cognition and feedback, a circular process of adaptation has created a unique auto-regulating, self-making system consisting of the biosphere and the Earth. Gaia is 'that' (the Hindu 'tat') and 'that' is change. **We, the planet and the biosphere - the Whole - change, or 'make ourselves' via cognition.**

Unlike other ecological theories, Gaia implies that the earth will survive our mismanagement, but that in adapting to it, as it has adapted to every change since its beginnings , it is likely to become an inhospitable place for humans. And that is because *Homo Faber* has broken with other living entities, who adapt to their environment.

The consciousness that individuals had of being of the Whole flowed from cognition and autopoiesis, both of which are associated with internal authority. Kauffman tells us that as it adapts to its environment, a cell does not know that it knows. Although humans do not always know *what* they know, it is because we know *that* we know, that we have an obligation to be responsible toward the Whole. It is the failure to recognize this, rather than a lack of specific knowledge, that could lead to our demise. For cognition can also be a blind process, not requiring mind. Without a certain level of consciousness, knowing that we know, or auto-referentiality can be a feedback loop that does not correct, but "anchors itself in concrete sense realities that give rise to judgement and 'ideas', impeding the flow of information and autopoiesis" (Zukav).

As humans began to transform their environment, they lost the internal authority that was part of being not only actors of the Whole, but intrinsically of the Whole, and society began to break down. As this was happening, psychology became systematized instead of being viewed as an unfinished area of self-making and adaptation. Echoing Lovelock, Kauffman notes that "networks near the edge of chaos appear best able to coordinate complex activities and to evolve, but are eventually driven to extinction by the collective behavior of the system as a whole." Hence the triple predicament of mankind: our inability to accept that life is sustained at the edge of chaos, that it is inevitably followed by death, and that the collective behavior of society does not always correspond to individual wisdom.

Biology, sociology and physics show that life is a globally near-equilibrium structure in constant transformation. Participatory democracy based on shared information would have a good chance of leading to successful phase transitions, but as suggested by Etzioni's theory of symbiosis (see Chapter II), it cannot lead to a permanent, 'stable' state. Lovelock too warns that humans must be aware of their link to the Whole in order for the Whole to remain in a state of symbiosis. At some point, failure to adapt destroys the advantageous state that is just far enough from equilibrium to be in balance.

In this chapter I have mentioned a few examples of the ways in which science confirms Taoism's basic intuition that, far from illustrating linear causality, the universe is a process of constant movement and transformation beyond that which can be apprehended by the intellect, even though information is at its heart. (The essentiality of information with respect to life confirms the anarchist intuition that education, learning, and internal authority - or autonomy - constitute the basic building blocks of civilization.)

But this chapter would be incomplete without a reference to the fact that The Big Bang too evokes the fundamental notions found in Hinduism, Buddhism and Taoism. The idea of an ongoing renewal can be represented either as a feedback loop, or as Bohm's enfolding and unfolding of matter. According to one theory, the universe consists of constant pulsations which alternately extend and contract (in other words, recompose) indestructible matter, with a Big Bang between each. According to Stephen Hawking, after *the* Big Bang, the universe continued to expand for about a million years until electrons and neutrons no longer had enough energy to overcome the electro-magnetic pull between them, at which point they began to combine, forming atoms.

Alternately cautious and ironic, Hawking's discussion of first cause leaves little doubt as to his position with respect to God: Positing three arrows of time, the thermodynamic, in which entropy increases, the psychological, which is the way humans experience time, and the cosmological, Hawking says it is only when they are related "that there can be intelligent beings who can ask the question (...)". In *The Constants of Nature*, Paul Barrows explains why intelligent beings can only exist in a universe with one time arrow and three space dimensions.

When all is said and done, theories about the Big Bang and synchronicity both refer back to Taoism. Listen again to Peat:

> The order of levels of order itself springs out of a creative source which must lie far beyond the orders of thought and matter; indeed it must be totally creative and absolutely unconditioned, beyond or-

ders of extreme speed and subtlety. But what then is
the nature of this source? To attempt to capture its
essence in thought or language would clearly be to
limit it. In the 6th century B.C.E., Lao Tzu wrote of
this source: 'The Tao which can be expressed in
words is not the unchangeable Tao. For if a name be
named it is not the unchangeable name. Without a
name it is the beginning of Heaven and Earth.

In other words, we must not adjectivize existence.
And Peat adds: "Some six hundred years later, the Roman philosopher Plotinus wrote: 'What is This which
does not exist? We can only go away silent, in utter
perplexity, and seek no further, for what could we look
for when there is nothing to go on? Every search points
to the First Principle and stops there.'"

Plotinus had a considerable and varied influence
on both Islamic and European thought up to the 17th
century, from Grotius, Erasmus and Giordano Bruno, to
Montaigne and Montesquieu, Blake, More, Descartes,
and Pascal, Spinoza and all manner of Pantheists. And
before Plotinus, there had been Epictetus, the foremost
Stoic, and Marcus Aurelius, the Emperor who applied
Epictetus' teachings not only to himself, but to his rule
over the second century Roman Empire. Epictetus, following Socrates and Diogenes, taught that there is only
one thing that fully belongs to an individual: his will, or
purpose, which cannot be thwarted by anything external. In other words, his conscience, or internal authority, man's only true freedom.

For me, Taoism's relevance stems from the fact
that it is a frame of mind rather than a dogma. Its principle source of reference, the *Tao Te Ching*, is only
5000 characters long, yet it still has meaning for us after almost 2,500 years. Taoists, Stoics, Neo-Platonists,

Deists and Romantics have all suspected that there is only One Main Idea, and that it requires neither rites nor priests. That idea, Unicity, winds like a thread through the fabric of every religion and school of thought. Although individuals disagree as to what it implies, it is an uninterrupted phenomenon.

With respect to dualism, the discussion revolves mainly around death. Is there a life after death? Is the soul separate from the body, and does it, at least, survive? Belief in the immortality of the soul stems from the hope of a better life after death, or even a new life, and religions use these aspirations to cajole us into becoming better in this life. I'm suggesting here that the findings of modern science, though fatal to dualists, nonetheless allow for a comforting view of mortality which in turn provides a cosmic foundation for responsibility:

If the universe and everything in it is made up of indestructible particles which eternally recompose, then the soul, consisting of the interplay of our senses, emotions and intellect, which we perceive but cannot see or touch, is one of the components of a unique being, like DNA or fingerprints, that involve the presence of indestructible - and hence immortal - particles. (Hawking notes that "If an astronaut falls into a black hole, its mass will increase. Eventually, the energy of that extra mass will be returned to the universe in the form of radiation. Thus, in a sense the astronaut will be recycled.")

It would appear that when we take away the idea of causality, we are left with the Hindu *tat tvam asi*, or 'that which is'. Our Self, our soul, which enfolds our senses, emotions and intellect, constitutes the seat of both our inalienable freedom, and our sense of responsibility, the sustained effort required by Ma'at to protect that-which-is. Perhaps the best way to get this idea across is to show it in the form of a feedback loop. The one below shows how the basic notions discussed here are linked to the material reality of human life, illustrating perhaps better than a series of sentences the relationship between the sacred, freedom and sustainable development, as promised earlier:

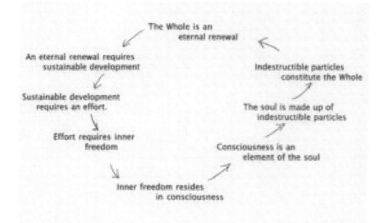

But how does this demonstration help to resolve our political challenges? Individuals realize that we must limit consumption of natural resources, yet society seems unable to implement the economic and cultural change this requires. We would increase humanity's chances of survival by recognizing that freedom, seated in consciousness, which is part of the Whole, must be constrained by Ma'at, the Rule, in order to protect the Whole.

Ultimately, we are faced with the task of ministering to a spirit battered by the ever more powerful products of the intellect. Of finding a way, without straightjacketing our minds, to bring a modicum of peace to a soul subjected to the closed political and technological systems our minds have created. This task requires respect for nature as a part of our selves, the acceptance of the Other for the same reason, and the use of technology to preserve and maintain the Whole, or Being. A healthy suspicion of knowledge and progress when, under pretext of objectivity, they usurp 'being with the world' by occupying a position outside it. Acceptance of death as an element of the ceaseless enfolding and unfolding of matter, and of the uninterrupted self-making that is the essence of life. A view of the universe based on complexity, order emerging from chaos and ceaseless transformations as the key to the renewal implied in autopoiesis, instead of the rigidities that have characterized most religious and scientific views.

In the North, "How does it work?" has enabled us to all but eliminate toil and achieve a maximum of comfort and health. But every day these benefits slip a bit further from our grasp. To enjoy them lastingly, and enable the South to enjoy similar benefits, we must accept that external freedom is limited by the nature of Being, that conscience is our only absolute freedom and that it demands responsibility. The ancients' "How does it work" led to dualism, while modern science leads to Unicity .

Our times require a sense of the sacred that inspires our behavior, rather than a religion that dictates it. Religion must be taught, thereby inevitably promoting dualism and intolerance of Otherness. Very differently, if not warped by intellectual constructs, a sense of the sacred in which human and environmental Otherness are inseparable from Self begets morality, making responsibility self-evident.

A transformation of our relationship to Otherness would be consistent with the scientific corpus we have given ourselves, and, far fetched as it may seem, enable us to deal with the economic predicament science has created: development versus ecological disaster.

XII
Sustainable Development...

When we Indians kill meat, we eat it all up.
When we dig roots, we make little holes.
We shake down acorns and pine nuts. We use
only dead wood. But the White people plow up the
ground, pull down the trees, kill everything.
Wintu Indian woman.

In this chapter we look at the economic and ecological imperative that underlies North/South violence. Cyrulnik draws attention to the emotional component of interpersonal violence as evidenced by comparisons with the animal world. But we are confronted now with a generalized violence that appears to be in all things, both material and immaterial, in our reactions to others, and our creations. Managing evolutive violence in an unbridled economic system is more complicated than in the past, involving not only relations within the polis and between the polis and its environment, but also between states, and between states and the global system.

The current unprecedented economic crisis has convinced a growing number of economists that growth must be 'sustainable'. However, it is not yet widely accepted that it must be radically curtailed in the North if the South is to achieve and maintain an acceptable standard of living. That is because power is no longer vested in states but in economic actors. As the South pursues Having, these actors fear it will contribute to the coming ecological catastrophe, yet they encourage it to move from an ordered society to a disordered one, from open-system cohabitation with nature to a closed system at war with the environment in the name of modernity. Responding to its lure, the South abandons a millennial social order as it allows the North to rape its treasures.

To ensure a reasonable and durable level of existence in all parts of the world, sustainable development would maintain a balance between the needs of man and those of his habitat, based on feedback. A classical example shows why this is essential. In a habitat shared by rabbits and foxes, the foxes feed on the rabbits. The more rabbits there are for them to eat, the larger the fox population grows. Soon the enlarged fox population has consumed so many rabbits that the rabbit population falls off, resulting in a corresponding drop in the fox population for want of food. When we behave like foxes, ignoring the feedback provided by cognition and consuming beyond our needs, we modify our relationship to the environment. Systems tend toward a steady state, but when feedback is ignored, entropy increases (the foxes die out).

Thinking we can solve our problems through growth, we persist in a linear 'more and more' instead of being content with a circular 'enough'. For the world system to survive, avoiding the overshooting and collapse predicted in *The Limits to Growth* and many works since, it must oscillate between order and disorder, avoiding both dissipation and entropy. Circles have a bad reputation in the West, as in 'going around in circles', 'a vicious circle', but in fact, the world does go around in circles, nature goes around in circles, and circles are not vicious, but virtuous, as 'primitive' peoples have always known. And they continue to impose themselves, for example the emerging tribal family, where spouses, ex-spouses and their various offspring are creating a new type of family tree in which hitherto extra-systemic relationships are integrated.

The question, then, is whether a New World Order will reflect linear Us/Them thinking, or development based on circular relations between states and a rethinking of the purpose of economics. Can we simply welcome the fastest growing countries into the OECD and line up together against the others? Those in which Islamic fundamentalism is often the dominant culture? If so, Samuel Huntington's *Clash of Civilizations* could lead to drones against migrants. But is his agenda the only answer to the six problem areas generally identified with the growing world crisis involving:

1. Ecology, i.e.: pollution, ozone;

2. The North/South divide: resources, population, food;

3. Nationalist aspirations based on religion and/or culture;

4. Civil conflicts between fundamentalists and modernists;

5. Migrations from underdeveloped to developed regions;

6. Disintegration of developed countries under the stress of unemployment, drugs, the death of the nuclear family and financial power.

The first thing we notice is that these interrelated challenges all stem from the promotion of Having over

Being. The disintegration of developed societies, religious, cultural, and developed/under-developed conflicts based on 'Us/Them' criteria, as well as South/North migrations, all flow from a linear mode of thinking that promotes Having over Being. As for the conduct of the financial sector, if it is not a result of mindless greed, we should consider the possibility that it may be part of a deliberate decision by those who run the world behind closed doors to continue milking the earth until they can colonize another planet, leaving a redundant 99% to their fate.

The application of circular thinking to economics would result in sustainable development in the South and slower growth in the North, allowing us to address the ecological imperative as well as our problem with Otherness. Sustainable/arrested development is the *sine qua non* condition for earth to remain a human habitat .

1. To protect the ozone layer, and avoid other types of pollution resulting from deliberate human choices and activities requires a switch to non-polluting, renewable sources of energy and consumer goods built to last.

2. The relationship between population and food is the most obvious example of interdependence. It highlights the deleterious effects of chemical fertilizers on the water table and food chain, the use of oil in their manufacture and the use of food as fuel. But feeding and caring for underdeveloped populations requires more than technology and money. It requires rethinking their needs together with the needs and habits of the developed world, so that decisions affecting the two populations are compatible, and respect the overall imperative of preserving our common habitat. In other words, it requires a balancing between life-giving dissi-

pation and entropy, between North and South, prosperous and developing economies.

3. Nationalist aspirations based on religion and/or culture are partly an outgrowth of inequality within Nation-states. Governments' fears of succession are partly due to the need to hold on to precious resources, good farmland, etc. In reality, this is only a problem as long as populations are organized into sovereign Nation-states. A focus on sustainable development shows that the creation of new states based on religious or cultural criteria is not a step backward if viewed as a counterpoint to the world-level organizations required to coordinate activities that could endanger our habitat. The international community purports to fear that small nations will lack sufficient resources to both be self-sufficient and bring in hard currency for trade. In reality they fear that too many cooks will spoil the broth of international affairs.

In 2012, eight cities had populations of over ten million (Tokyo had thirty-eight and New York nineteen). If cities become as populous as as some Nation-states, we must rethink sovereignty and government. How could planners hope to maintain cities within reasonable limits, if not by dividing them into neighborhoods with accountable governments linked to regional and supranational institutions? (The Brazilian city of Curitiba is a pioneer in decentralization.)

4. The fundamentalist/modernist antagonism results from a growing aversion to the type of societies the developed world has built up in its pursuit of Having. A rethinking of the idea of all-out freedom and consumerism will allow Islamic societies to modernize peacefully and sustainably, while decentralization will

enable them to retain their attachment to community. Opposition to consumer capitalism has manifested itself in places as diverse as Turkey and Brazil.

5. Migratory trends are due to lack of jobs in the underdeveloped world, which is linked to the way resources are allocated on the basis of countries' buying power, as well as to prices paid for raw materials and produce. Unemployment is unlikely to disappear as long as resources go mainly to areas that are already rich and prices are set to make them richer. In the first graph, the south's raw materials go North, where they are trans-formed into products. Payments go to the upper classes, who also purchase the North's products, while the poor, left out of the process, flow northward, causing some unemployment and weighing on welfare systems. Without pointing the finger at money, the second, more circular graph suggests that when interactions flow from the most basic entity, resources, joining North and South in an open, dynamic system, points of friction are reduced.

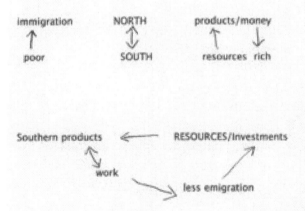

For the foreseeable future, migratory trends must be treated by target countries as inevitable, since sustainable development requires populations to be distributed over the various regions of the earth in accordance with their respective carrying capacities. Where geographic conditions do not permit sustainable development, populations will continue to seek survival elsewhere. Australia, New Zealand, the United States, Canada, certain parts of Africa, have large under-populated areas. Insofar as they exhibit sufficient carrying capacity (space being but one criterion), they will be immigrant destinations. Jeffrey Sachs, who has moved slightly to the left in recent years, described the role of geography in the development process, concluding that the North must resign itself to increasing migration. The movement of Western Chinese into Siberia would suggest that Russia and China already accept that reality, while Europe, goaded by powerful Neo-fascist parties, tries in vain to stem African immigration.

6. Disintegration of developed countries under the stress of unemployment, drugs, and the death of the nuclear family results in the marginalization of those for whom automation has no jobs. As I shall show in the next chapter, the redefinition of work consonant with the needs of a planet that rejects Having for Having's sake, would eliminate unemployment and reduce crime and drugs.

Progress defined as unlimited consumption is incompatible with a steady state economy, depleting resources and breeding violence. And yet, sustainable development is still not a worldwide aspiration. When Northern decision makers began to realize that the earth was living beyond its means in terms of pollution, agricultural capacity and renewable resources, they declared that the South would have to adopt strict family planning, and even, then it should not expect to reach the quality of life that exists in the North. At the Rio Conference on the Environment in 1992, in Kyoto in 1997 and in Copenhagen in 2009, the South was asked to limit its energy use in order to avoid increasing industrial pollution. Obviously this request was poorly received by southern governments.

In a related phenomenon, southern governments resent the North's ethnocentric demand that they respect fundamental human rights when their people have yet to enjoy the material conditions that allow them to care about values. It took us several centuries to arrive at the exaggeration of political correctness, yet we expect countries where women wash their clothes in a stream to share our intellectual approach to life. Arguing over the extent to which under-development is a result of colonialism, Western governments fail to see the need to balance resources and populations. Not even September 11 made the point: we focused our attention on terrorism instead of its causes. Recent research into bio-history and bio-geography can help us see things more clearly.

XIII
....And Bio-Geography

Luminous nature, passionate nature,
mysterious nature emanates from me;
but I am not in them, they are in me.
Baghavad Gita

In his widely read *Guns, Germs and Steel*, Jared Diamond, a geo-biologist who rejected compartmentalization to become a historian and anthropologist, describes the specific bio-geological conditions that prevailed on Earth from as far back as 11,000 B.C.E., and which, through a fascinating series of interactions, played a role in the development of inequalities between various regions of the globe. Combining archeological evidence with the observation of contemporary primitive societies, Diamond shows that the first major progress-fostering development, i.e., the transition from hunting-gathering to agriculture, took place earliest in the Fertile Crescent and other central latitudes, especially those with Mediterranean type climates.

Investigating why the transition did not take place in all parts of the world at the same time, Diamond found that the crucial factors were differing types of indigenous wild food and animal strains, climate, and population densities. Describing the successive interactions that led to the present gap between North and South, Diamond shows why at certain times various civilizations could conquer neighbors, while at others they declined.

From the height of our two-thousand year civilization, 'the past' is scarcely older than that. But if we want to know how we got where we are, we have to look at early human communities. Engels studied them during his early collaboration with Marx, but we know a lot more now than he could then. Contemporary political leaders should realize that if inequality between nations developed over thousands of years, with environmental factors having been decisive, improving that situation cannot merely be a question of ideology.

Retracing the evolution from hunter-gatherer societies to the present, Jared Diamond describes the basic structure of organized society, which for too long now has been hidden by ideological spin: kleptocracy, a monopoly of information and decision-making, an official police, the use of money, the existence of cities, the presence of rich and poor. Unless a cultural transformation allows us to modify this structure, we shall not be able to improve the North/South relationship and the violence it fosters.

Diamond's analysis brings us back to the problem of external authority. About a million years ago, bands of five to eighty nomads, each consisting of several extended families, spread into Eurasia from Africa. They held territory in common and had an informal leadership based on personality, physical strength, intelligence and fighting skills. Everyone, including children, hunted or foraged for food. By around 11,000 B.C.E., groups in the Fertile Crescent had expanded into tribes of several hundred. They lived in fixed settlements made possible by a concentration of food resources, especially wild cereals. Kinship groups or clans all held equal rank, each owned part of the land, and information and decision-making were shared. No tribe could become richer than another because they had reciprocal debts and obligations, in what long remained an exchange economy. Since everyone knew everyone else, conflicts could be resolved without an organized police: relatives or friends intervened to prevent bloodshed between parties to a dispute.

Around 5,500 B.C.E., when tribes reached several thousand, it became more difficult to solve disputes informally. Since the parties might not have common friends or relatives, a centralized police force was necessary. Still, shared beliefs continued to help unrelated people live together through bonds other than kinship, and even to sacrifice their lives for each other. Food storage enabled the group to feed more people than those required for production, and thus to maintain not only artisans and police, but hereditary chiefs and shamans. These latter had a monopoly on information and the use of force, and employed large numbers of bureaucrats to keep everyone in line. Taxes were instituted in the form of tribute, whose redistribution in popular ways also helped chiefs stay on top and retain however much of it they wanted for themselves. The chiefs and shamans claimed to serve the people through what Diamond calls a hot line to the Gods, while disarming them, arming the elite, and using their monopoly of force to curb violence.

It was at this stage of human development that the basic problem of civilized society appeared: how much of the tribute extracted from producers can be safely retained by the elite, and to what extent do producers approve the use made of the rest? Diamond points out that the difference between a wise statesman and a kleptocrat is merely one of degree, and the rest may well be idle chatter - whether over the Internet or by tam-tam.

Diamond's investigations show that specialization and compartmentalization began very early in human history, with the creation of a recognized external authority that called in non-concerned parties to regulate violence. Seven thousand years later, we have attained a degree of compartmentalization that guarantees total disagreement as to how tribute is redistributed, with Mafia-like governments increasing the use of signs that transgress the laws of nature and emphasizing violence.

In addition to being ruled by oligarchies, populations today are increasingly subjected to intermediaries. When in primitive societies the chief took in the surplus agricultural product, redistributing it to bureaucrats and artisans, or to the entire population in the off season, or storing it for emergencies, the food producers paid one level of intermediaries in order to benefit from the services of all. Today, there are countless levels of intermediaries that farmers and other producers are required to pay, in addition to donating a share of their production to government through taxes. This situation forces them to raise their prices, eventually resulting in disaffection and lack of responsibility among the rest of the population. In societies where government demands ever greater contributions from taxpayers for projects they often do not approve, individual behavior degenerates into a form of hostage-taking, each doing less and less, while demanding ever greater rewards, in a pervasive violence that has no winners.

In the United States, although medical insurance is beginning to be recognized as a right, obscene profits dramatically increase the cost of care, while foreign wars take budgetary priority. Since the majority of citizens did not choose this situation, it would probably be fair to say that representative democracy is a more or less hopeless attempt to manage what is in fact a generalized anarchy, as the system oscillates ever more wildly between order and disorder.

As part of a reconquest of internal authority, post-scarcity democracy must acquire individually based control not only of taxation but also of administration. To create an equilibrium between North and South that nature has not provided will require employment and consumption policies that can achieve a more balanced distribution of goods and less pollution. This can only happen if both first world habits and third world needs are taken into account, something only an international body can do.

Kleptocratic government may have been necessary to get from there to here, but having seen that 'here' is a dead end, we need to change the way we redistribute the value generated by human activity, not according to an ideology, but by replacing kleptocracy as an unavoidable fact of government with collective decision-making based on information processed by individuals cognizant of their own internal authority. What is most important is not that hunter-gatherer societies were egalitarian in the economic sense, but that they were truly anarchical: there was no formal chief and no priest, at best a leader of the hunt. Hierarchical external authority did not appear until bands became tribes, then chiefdoms, and men had to learn how to meet strangers without killing them.

The hunter-gatherer whose trajectory from Africa to the four corners of the earth Diamond traces was the same biologically as we are, however violence today is experienced under far greater concentrations of populations than those of prehistoric times. This is due in part to the abandonment of religion in favor of a rationality that has no place for spirituality, and a lack of rituals that mitigate our representations of Others.

During the Enlightenment, Europeans became convinced that by rejecting the authority of the church they could develop their rational capabilities. In doing so they hastened the renouncement of internal authority that had begun with the advent of agriculture, increasingly leaving decisions to an elite and eventually alienating their inner freedom to the concept of nation. Kleptocrats told their subjects that the democratic Nation was 'theirs'. But gradually, bureaucrats, from underlings, became the new rulers.

Culture enabled society to progress. Now it causes it to regress by disconnecting it from the Whole, as cognition no longer serves self-making, but breeds alienation instead. Information is more widely available, but it focuses on Having instead of Being. When humans sought to improve their situation vis a vis nature, life had a direct meaning which linked them to the Whole. With its varying degrees of kleptocracy, concentration of information and decision-making, civilization has led to a completely auto-referential society, separating humans from their environment and from

each other, ejecting the meaning of life from the circular orbit of the Whole like a satellite lost in space.

As Watts described it:

> Modern culture is like a painting on a wall. It al-
> lows us to talk about it, while forbidding us to pene-
> trate it. Religion, poetry, and music have become
> mere ornaments of our minds, a spectacle to be rel-
> ished, but not an active fete, meaningful and unify-
> ing. Having ceased to believe in the old myths,
> modern man tries to invent new ones: the automo-
> bile, money, publicity, information, computers. Or
> health, which has become a permanent right, old
> age and death being regrettable mistakes of nature -
> or the result of poor political analysis.

Watts' analysis could not be convincing to his con-
temporaries because they could not add the notion of
internal authority to poetry and knowledge. Happily,
recent geographical, anthropological and psychological
research allows us to insert the counter-culture's intui-
tions into a scientific framework, and to recognize that
besides being unpoetic, Manichean analysis does not
improve matters. Given the permanence of the order/
disorder dyad, symbiosis invariably gives way to antagonism when one element of the dyad becomes durably
stronger than the other. As intuited by the Taoists and
modern science, when the urge to fix things interferes
with counter-balancing, the system becomes antagonistic, with negative feedback increasing disorder and entropy.

Modern technology has led to carbon-dating and
the detailed analysis of soils, which tell the story of
human evolution. But it cannot replace the ability of
mind to comprehend the significance of information.
Computer models can help only if they are part of a

movement away from compartmentalization, which they can exacerbate. Many disciplines need be involved if we are to figure out where we want to go from here and how to get there, including psychology and sociology, helping internal authority to focus on Other-acceptance.

Although the internet encourages people to buy things they do not need, by saving time and energy, it also frees them to do other things. In *The End of Work* Jeremy Rifkin affirms that volunteer initiatives must do the jobs that neither the state nor the market will fund. Working fewer hours for a paycheck will leave time for meaningful engagement in the community, allowing children to participate with parents in its projects. By following his suggestions we could refound modern society on a basis that brings back other positive aspects of tribal culture such as gift-giving. But as long as we accept external authority, we shall lack the tools required to overcome 3,000 years of social compartmentalization.

The valorization of internal authority will enable us to affirm a meaning of life that links us to the Whole and reorganize the means by which we support it. Fundamentalists of all stripes demand greater subservience to external authority, but it is greater internal authority that will enable us to reclaim our place within the Whole. At present, we do not invent things in order to improve our relationship to Others, but merely to make money, an end in itself. We assume that unemployment and competition are inevitable because we view civilizations that lack them as inferior. The signs related to this attitude transgress the laws of nature, since they are part of a closed system that stands outside it. And as we remove ourselves from the environment, the Other removes himself from us.

No one in his right mind would wish to turn the clock back to the time of Cyrulnik's hunter, for whom "every moment of life was filled with affectivity and meaning, until the moment of death, which came early." But the hunter also remarked that "white men who work unceasingly merely to garner a subsistence are probably less happy than he, resting comfortably, after meeting all his needs in the pleasure of hunting and fishing". We do not want to live by candlelight or die of pneumonia, but neither do we want our children to overdose.

Autopoiesis gave rise to a species that was capable of abstract thinking, culture and auto-referentiality, and could 'extract itself from the context'. This enabled it to dominate and to judge. Now humans must adapt to each Other, learning to live not in a clan, but side by side with neighbors who are total strangers. We take this arrangement for granted, yet in evolutionary terms, it represents an enormous trauma to which we have yet to adapt. There is a growing worldwide movement toward small communities, but thus far it does not appear to have sparked a call for global coordination of sustainable development, reversing the giant feedback loop that began when hunter-gatherers became farmers.

Scientific awareness should enable both the Judeo-Christian world and Islam to explore their own past and each other's, according to new definitions of needs and morality that would allow both to elaborate a future based on what is best in each. Islamic fundamentalists fail to criticize their own past, and now they are confronted with our present. Values and ways of life that we left behind are also contained in the Qu'ran, and those who are drawn to Islam value the spirit of community it propounds. (Similarly, in Eastern Europe, a significant number of citizens have shown by their vote that they appreciated the economic security provided by Communist governments that tried, by way of a centralized system, to implement solidarity.) The notion of Oneness, or Unicity, could diffuse the threat of fundamentalism and limit migration to what Northern carrying capacity can bear as it encourages the South's development on its own terms.

We have always believed that the present represents progress with respect to every past, and that the future would be better still. We forgot that 'better', a typically linear notion, is sometimes the enemy of the good; but a society organized in pursuit of sustainable development starts to move away from the one in which the grandchildren of Marcuse believe that total liberty is the best thing since sliced cheese, to one in which they value their inner freedom, the closeness of family and friends, and the sense of belonging to a community, where their need for action can be appreciated. In which not only remunerated work, but also contributions of time and effort to a community's overall quality of life, are taken into account in the allocation of financial rewards and social standing. People who know they have a place in society do not require drugs.

The disintegration of the family may take a long time to overcome, but society will adjust to the new role of women and the extended families that result from serial divorces. The decision of the Madres de Mayo to no longer pin their children's picture on their lapels, but to affirm that each is the mother of all those who were killed, prefigures a society in which children are every-one's responsibility, thus protecting them from the selective disregard of external bureaucratic authority.

We need to recognize that we can live better if we accept the unending circle of life and death, organizing our economic life to take account of the repercussions of all things on all others. For that we shall have to re-invent the economic system that has delivered us from labor, but still holds us in bondage.

XIV
Marginal Improvements

Do not break bread if you see some-
one is in need and you are not helping
him. Last year's rich man is now a
stable boy. For the waters this year
took a different course.
Ancient Egyptian Proverb

Although the meaning of work has changed over time, men continue to demand it because it is the only thing they know. Work used to be part of Being, now it is about 'Having' or 'Not-Having'. Originally, work sustained individuals directly; gradually, it became a mediated phenomenon: individuals hire themselves out in order to acquire goods produced by other individuals. From a personal activity, work was transformed into a means of exchange, and eventually we discovered that the system can go berserk. Having been persuaded to buy superfluous products on credit, when we lose employment we cannot meet our basic needs

Primitive man, seeing that there was nothing more to gather or hunt in a given place, moved on. But when the basis for work-as-survival is a mediated process, men can only shout their despair. When they transformed work from a relationship with the environment to a relationship with others, they lost the internal authority that had enabled them to control their daily lives. Their survival is contingent upon those for whom

Being is Having, who can consume whether others work or not.

We may wonder how can there still be poverty in such a highly developed a civilization as ours. How can it be that even governments are in debt? What has happened since the time, only thirty years ago, when Westerners produced and consumed, and the gap between rich and poor was much smaller? In the previous chapter, we noted the role played by intermediaries, but obsolescence is the biggest culprit: endless investments are required to create new products and ever newer versions of existing products, the cycle repeated over and over again in order to sell more units of what is essentially the same item, producing marginal improvements that feed obsolescence. Labor may be the largest single element involved, but when taken together, the other costs total more.

We're told that prices have 'gone up', but we're never told that the reason is obsolescence. When the modern economy was being born, in the fifties in the United States, or in the sixties and seventies in Western Europe, there were fewer companies making ovens and fewer types of ovens (mini oven, micro-wave, combination, grill, etc.). Although the standard of living for Western populations was increasing, and consumer goods were becoming widespread as the ratio of production costs to wage levels allowed more and more people to consume, housewives were not clamoring for GE to produce an endless variety of ovens. Yet GE did just that.

The costs of planned obsolescence start with the idea for a 'new' oven, then a design by an engineer who has a support staff, equipment, etc. Then comes the investment in machines to manufacture the oven, and finally, the oven must be packaged for shipment to all parts of the country and the world.

Or take the number of people behind a simple box of detergent. In addition to the R & D budget required to come up with an ever 'new and improved' product, there are line workers and office workers, a multinational corporation with plants all over the world, a director of communications, a million dollar advertising budget involving local market research teams, sales teams and a headquarters building designed by a major architect. The end result is fewer jobs and ever greater quantities of dirty clothes. Since line jobs have almost all been automated, most of the labor bill is spent on white collar jobs, but when unemployment is high, all workers consume less beyond their basic needs. And when one worker loses his job, another bears the added cost of his unemployment benefits, thus also consuming less. If society stopped producing marginal improvements(a soap for wool, a soap for color, a soap with softener in it, etc.), more people would have clean clothes.

Obsolescence was facilitated by and simultaneously made finance the driver of economic activity. Ever larger sums of money generated by complex financial manipulations needed somewhere to go. At the height of this system, lured by the promise of high returns, banks all over the world invested in toxic assets that lead to collapse. Putting this situation into a larger context, what the modern world calls 'full employment' has had but a brief history. For most of his existence man lived at one level of remove from the products he consumed, intervening on animals or plants with his bare hands or basic tools. Two hundred years ago in

France, workers used simple machines to transform natural substances for the benefit of a privileged few, who lived at three levels of remove from fine products. Workers and peasants were left with just enough to survive (and produce), and inflation was kept to a tolerable level by periodic revolts, droughts, wars, famines and epidemics.

With the industrial revolution came Man>Nature->Capital->Machines->Product, putting the consumer at four levels of remove from the things he consumed. In the early stages, those who worked were still not the same people as those who spent, their wages being insufficient, while those who consumed did not have to work. In the mid-20th century, the developed world reached a tentative equilibrium in which the wages of producers became sufficient for some discretionary spending. At the same time, industrial wealth having replaced land wealth, those who had previously consumed without working, went to work, in the better paying jobs requiring the prolonged schooling that replaced the ancient privilege of birth.

When competition gradually became the principle motor of Western society, it transformed what was a relatively balanced situation into a frenzy driven by fabricated wants. It's no longer a question of getting more land through battle, but of selling more things. This requires that advertising turn from informing: ("We made this, which does that"), to creating desire: ("Buy this and you will be happy!"). In the rush to meet every whim created by advertising, manufacturing became more capital intensive (ideas + machines), while requiring ever less labor.

This system extends to governments, social services and NGOs - as well as to the cost of producing a modern adult: Mr. Middle American Taxpayer pays property taxes, most of which are used to defray the cost of operating his children's schools. This cost has soared because schools are now loaded with products of marginal benefit, such as 'teaching packages', learning devices, wall to wall carpeting, etc., which the little red schoolhouse did very well without while teaching kids to read and write better than schools do now. Not only do these marginal improvements cost more than what tax revenues can buy, without them, teachers could be better paid, and classes could be much smaller.

Health costs too have soared, not so much because people are getting better care, but because care is now administered via a host of marginal improvements How many deaths have been avoided thanks to improvements in the operating room equipment involved in appendectomies? A visit to any doctor or lab reveals an endless stream of what can only be called 'gadgets', while the ultimate marginal benefit is the exaggerated extension of human life that banishes death beyond the horizon of Never-Never Land.

Turning now to expenditures related to administration and control, every consumer spends a percentage of his income, in the form of taxes, to remunerate those who oversee the aides provided by government to alleviate the distress caused by the system of marginal improvements. Employing people to ensure that no one is cheating is probably more costly than were the money used to automatically pay an honest wage to both groups. (For several decades a movement calling for a guaranteed income independent of work has been gaining ground in Europe, however it is virtually unknown in the United States.)

Limits to Growth warned against overshooting, the continuation of a trend beyond its real limits, followed by bifurcation into collapse. From the one-on-one existence of the first immigrants from Africa to the Fertile Crescent, we have overshot to a billion-on-billion electronic existence that involves endless middlemen and the manipulation of money. The amount it takes to produce and maintain a human being is now at least 1,000 times higher than, say, in the Middle Ages, and although she does not directly produce, and cannot possibly afford to consume 1000 times more direct products than her ancestors, she does produce 1,000 times more by using machines. If we measure her consumption by the common denominator of energy (to which everything can ultimately be reduced), she also consumes 1,000 times more, an aberration that now endangers the planet. (Recent findings suggest that there have been times in the past when climate change has come suddenly, and this could again be the case, as each year brings more violent weather phenomena, largely a result of excessive CO_2 in the atmosphere.)

Until recently, economists believed that higher growth rates and global coordination would lead to a significant cut in work hours and increased leisure, however it turns out that growth puts many out of work. The world has sufficient resources and technology for both developed and under-developed populations to live reasonably well if growth is managed. But humans have for so long feared scarcity that the idea of limiting growth was anathema until the austerity imposed by the

2008 financial crisis brought the system to the brink of collapse.

In *Prosperity without Growth*, the Australian economist Tim Jackson focuses exclusively on the developed world, where a key step toward de-growth would be to drastically reduce transportation costs. At a time when agriculture and industry can produce almost anything anywhere, what is the sense of, say, France importing Spanish melons, or even more illogically, ordinary British tableware? Serge Latouche in *The End of Growth* calls for the over-developed parts of the planet to abandon planned obsolescence and return Africa's minerals to the control of its governments. Africans are not only deprived of the revenues from their vast mineral wealth, agricultural land is being bought up by foreign entities as a hedge against food shortages, causing local hunger. The continent's economic growth rate is much higher than the developed world's, however in a rush to modernize, traditional people have left sustainable communities for urban slums. Like a growing number of thinkers, Latouche believes that Africans could rebuild sustainable indigenous economies, taking only what is truly life-enhancing from modernity and returning to traditional morality, self-respect and community.

In *From the Ruins of Empire*, Pankaj Mishra reminds us that the oriental cultures only adopted 'progress' once they came under our influence, and currently, the very concepts which for millennia held them back, are being revived in a world-wide revolt against consumerism. While Turkish youth occupied Istanbul's main park slated to become a shopping mall, Brazilians demonstrated against the cost of hosting the World

Football Cup. European young people, especially in the southern countries hit hardest by the financial crisis, have begin to leave the cities for small towns and villages. American workers too are discovering that the 'dream' is just that, making escalating tuition costs a bad investment when 3D printing machines can produce almost anything people need. Although the first 3D printed item to be marketed in the U.S. was a gun, thanks in part to social media, solidarity is gaining ground and people across the world realize that a system has only one pot, demanding that in the existing system profits be plowed back into it via taxes to meet the housing, health care, eduction, and leisure needs of all.

These unforeseen phenomena suggest that the 20th century is only now really coming to an end, the teens ushering in a new era, as they did a century ago. As the production of ever more stuff brings oil and other 'peaks', credit adds yet another level of separation between consumer and product. Capital and technology, while liberating man from toil and creating ever more 'pleasures' for him to enjoy, impoverish individuals, countries, and even the international institutions set up to protect us from war and other global catastrophes.

In prehistoric times, before work became separated from play (which is part of, Being), it produced at the same time goods and satisfactions, as we are reminded by Cyrulnik's Indian. When work ceased to be play in the sense of a challenging, satisfying experience, consumption was brought in. We need to realize that since we consume to compensate for toil, we could, thanks to technology, work less and also consume less, while producers, no longer forced to engage in a competitive struggle for survival would have less reason to pursue endless marginal improvements. Three hundred years ago, Louis XVI's chemist and tax collector, Lavoisier, who pioneered the metric system, noted that "Economics is balance. Nothing is lost, nothing is created."

Since external authority is no longer used to force people to work, but to consume, we must ask ourselves whether growth for endless consumption is the answer to our question about the meaning of life. Should we accept external authority to the point of denying not only our freedom to think, but our responsibility to maintain the Whole? We do not require growth to ensure the necessities of life, but to enable more people to consume ever more things, depriving the producers of basic goods of their subsistence. Ten thousand years after hunters settled down, the technological progress that began with the choice to cultivate food and build shelters has led us to a cramped summit with loose rocks under foot.

Prehistoric man required external authority to ensure a regular supply of food and obtain greater security vis a vis the Other. Now, to survive, we need to cultivate our inner authority and move further along the evolutionary path, adapting to the-Other-as-part-of-the-Whole, recognizing that 'things' may make life easier or more pleasurable, but they do not provide meaning.

To bridge the gap between the haves and the have-nots, our relationship with the world around us is more relevant than power. The philosopher Paul Ricoeur affirms that the more power man has, the more problems he creates. That is 'the way things are', for power begets action, and action begets reaction. Rather than not acting, we need to act in different ways, on different parts of the problématique. Many scientists, whatever their religious orientation, now consider that human life cannot go on if spiritual needs remain unmet. An ecological economic system would reflect a society moving away from the linear concept of God-as-Supreme-Other - above and outside of man - toward the circular concept that all life partakes of the same sacredness because it is One. The awareness that man is a part - or even an aspect - of nature should enable us to create sustainable economies and develop Other-acceptance.

Fighting today's battles with yesterday's weapons, speculative globalization touts competition at a time when it is no longer justified by the struggle for survival, providing an excessive quality of life to the few while ensuring misery for the many. All should benefit from 'progress' without being ruled by it, enjoying cultural enrichment and tending to the needs of the polis, which even under the best of circumstances are unending.

XV
Universal History and the Imperative Alliance

*There is a great danger that anyone who
casts doubt on an abstract political universalism
(code for world government) will be called all
the names that modernity has anathematized.*
Tim Jackson

People argue over different kinds of political systems. However, the growing militarization of the police in the U.S. - which is likely to be followed by a similar trend in other countries - raises the question of whether people should allow governments to abuse the use of force. Instead of arguing over the reasons for which force is used, we need to realize that it is the abandonment of individual internal authority that allows external authorities to abuse their monopoly on force.

Increasing numbers of people around the world now understand that both capitalism and communism are driven by the same assumption that man is outside of nature. They believe we should no longer see nature as an enemy to be vanquished, but approach it in a spirit of peaceful co-existence, like the Wintu Indian woman quoted at the head of Chapter V. That means ensuring sustainability by using only what is needed for healthy, satisfying lives, knowing that growth cannot go on forever on a finite planet. Being able to do this does not depend on ownership of the means of production or even forms of government, but on individual awareness. The word 'citizen' hides the fact that even the most democratic government not only controls, but defines the existence of its members, imposing its will to the extent permitted by them. Therefore, the choice should not be between capitalism and socialism, but in favor of maximum participation by citizens in the decisions that affect their lives.

If Varela and Maturana are right that life doesn't consist of things, but of interactions that take place through the processing of information; and if Capra is right that information results in self-organization and self-making, then Chomsky's assertion that history is powered by the need for recognition, as well as Hegel/Fukuyama's conflict between greed and rebellion, are only partly relevant. Marx's thesis and antithesis can be translated as order/disorder, with synthesis being equal to a far from equilibrium, or stable state. Marx could not know that a stable state eventually dissipates either into disorder/entropy, or a higher level of order/complexity, meaning that no synthesis can be definitive. Similarly, Fukuyama notwithstanding, history will not be 'over' until humanity is.

To avoid self-inflicted extinction, we need to see history as an unending series of disruptions and bifurcations that will never achieve 'It', however hard we try. We can only influence processes, knowing that there is no final point, no perfect world which we shall be able to sit back and enjoy once we have created it. Aside from the intolerable dullness of such an eventuality, it isn't going to happen.

Although order/disorder is the way things are, technology enables us to generate a reasonable income for everyone on the planet with very little work, freeing time for the participatory democracy that corporatocracy cannot deliver. Neither democracy granted as a counter-weight to kleptocracy nor birth control have done away with poverty: structured by external authority, it endures. Solidarity is an emanation of internal authority, as shown in pre-kleptocratic societies where births were self-regulated to preserve the group from famine. And aside from the decisive role played by money in modern governance, efforts to manage edge-of-chaos phase transitions through external authority will always fail, because bureaucratic directives cannot be fine-tuned. Only a society of internally free individuals can make the constant minute adjustments required to durably maintain the system Earth in a relatively stable state.

The nation-state is only a few hundred years old, but it has been so closely associated with civilization that we cannot conceive of one without the other. And yet, secessionist movements show that people prefer to live among their own kind rather than in multi-national entities. After six hundred years of antagonism, Serbs and Kosovars cannot be expected to live side by side as the universalist West would like them to. Similarly, the odds are not favorable that Sunnis, Shi'as and Kurds can live together without strongmen like Saddam Hussein in charge. Recognizing the human need for a familiar immediate environment is an economic and ecological necessity, as well as a step up on the evolutionary ladder. When the world is seen as one vast community, made up of many homogeneous local communities, with world culture a counterpoint to the infinite variety of local cultures, humans will be less likely to view neighbors as 'Others'.

During World War I, European socialists tried to tell conscripts that their respective working classes had more in common with each other than with their rulers, imploring them to desert. Tragically, a century of nationalism had convinced those on either side that it was better to be governed by their own rulers than by foreign ones: relinquishing their internal authority, they went to the slaughter. Following that conflict, the nation-state and capitalism grew up together, and now 'citizens' not only fight the state's battles, as 'consumers' rather than as 'citizens', they buy what the businessmen who run the state tell them to.

When we added The Nation to our pantheon of Gods, we thought it would bring us happiness if we identified with it. Over time, we allowed it to take over the role of God-as-Absolute, its absoluteness, like that of God, based on its Otherness. Accepting the idea that the world is separated into many parts, we ceased being with the Whole and regulating our actions accordingly. If belonging to the whole were more important than belonging to a nation, it would not require a vote of the Security Council to stop massacres. An international force has no stake in a dispute, making intervention in the affairs of sovereign states as logical as local police who settle individual disputes. World governance is the only acceptable external authority because it corresponds to Gaia, the system as a whole. As such it would be the administration of things called for by Marx, relaying basic guidelines to the participatory democratic instances of local communities.

September 11th was the breaking point in a far-from-equilibrium situation that political systems will be unable to control until the world stabilizes at a 21st century level of development. Both those who favor all-out 'war on terror' and those who would oppose peace and love to the world's disparities, are trying to solve today's problems with yesterday's paradigms. We don't need to chase down every terrorist, nor try to put globalization back in the bottle. To diminish the influence of Bin Laden's successors, we need a different kind of globalization that coordinates the wants and needs of all parts of the system, including our habitat.

In the chapter on sustainable development, we saw that redistribution of resources and people is a major factor in development: it's useless to teach men to fish if all the fish have been caught upstream. On the other hand, peak resources and pollution forbid worldwide adoption of the North's extravagant lifestyle. For the South to accept sustainable development and the North to manage its status as world minority with minimal bloodshed, the latter will have to limit its upstream catch of the former's resources and adopt new lifestyles.

As things now stand, we feel helpless, and blame this or that party or country for the crises that cascade across the world. If we could see the universe as a whole, we would realize that man must answer, not to separating entities such as states or parties, but to himself as part of that Whole, the way tribal societies did for eons. We would realize that wars and movements for liberation or succession, emanate from the same aspiration towards equity that has always motivated humans.

Instead of expending energy on discrete events, we would favor processes that move the planetary system toward cohesive development, renewing the alliance that once existed between man and nature and creating interpersonal rituals that prevent violence. Until we question basic assumptions about authority, we will be forced to submit to the linear, hegemonist rituals of the financial-military-industrial complex that constitutes the worldwide ruling minority.

Interestingly, affirming individual authority means overcoming the opprobrium of so-called 'mob rule'. When you think about it, mobs represent the cumulative energy of myriad individual internal authorities, the faith of a cohort of individuals in their ability to know what's right and to demand that it be done. In a stunning feedback loop inspired by victories of left-wing governments in Latin America, the Latino community has joined with American blacks and Native Americans to demand a Rooseveltian commitment to support the working class. Barack Obama's failure to allow them to 'make him' do what's right led to the Occupy Movement that spread across the world, confirming the birth of a new era.

We need to visualize three worlds: the planet ten thousand years ago, when humans first began to form large communities; the one we inhabit today, in which a minority whose agenda is all about Having takes advantage of the majority, and the one we must achieve if humanity is to be durably supported by nature. We dispose of considerable means, lacking only that sense of the sacred that could bridge the gap between believers and skeptics and serve as a basis for public and private morality.

Michael Ignatieff dismissed the idea that human beings should be considered sacred, claiming we cannot use religion to justify human rights because this would not convince non-believers. But sacredness does not derive from God, it derives from the sacredness of all living things, (which I refer to as the Whole), and non-believers should be able to buy into that idea. A politics based on the notion of sacredness as affirmed by modern science is what I call a Taoist politics. It would accept that there is no such thing as reversibility and that humans can only try to influence bifurcations. Accepting that life consists of constant change, meaning that nothing is forever, including preferred outcomes, Taoist-inspired political activity would focus on the need to organize the planet so that ten billion people will be able to share its resources and manage their reciprocal Otherness with minimal external authority.

However difficult it may be for social activists to admit this, when the downtrodden jump the fence, they too subjugate, exploit, deceive, rape, and pillage; for greed, envy, and lust for power are present in all of us. And when we transform reaching for preferred outcomes into combat to achieve them, we struggle against one of the two elements of life - Yang - instead of recognizing it as part of ourselves. Happily, unlike a belief in 'God' or 'Truth', recognition of the is-ness, or sacredness, of Life, Yin/Yang, or the Whole, fosters awareness of both individual internal authority and the imperative of justice on the part of external authorities.

No less, instead of allowing governments to maintain linear, dominators/dominated relations with each other, we can require that they tend toward Ma'at. Unlike the sovereignty of kings, emperors and presidents that misuses nature and Others, Pharaoh's sovereignty represented a truly cosmic order, a feedback loop in which, as beneficiaries of the Gods, men continuously returned their blessings through him and their respect of the Rule. In that context, death was not merely inseparable from life; it was inconceivable that there could be another place for it to exist than within the dense cosmic Whole.

Manifestations of Yin/Yang, the Whole, or order/ disorder, as well as the expected and unexpected consequences of their interactions are beyond human control, leading to bifurcations that are largely unpredictable. That is why we do not so much need an external authority such as a Prime Minister or a President, as we need Ma'at, the rule that flows from awareness that disorder existed before the Gods, and that Being is the only absolute. The Egyptians knew instinctively what Stuart Kauffman and other scientists have deduced using sophisticated intellectual tools: that if he negates the Whole, man cannot guarantee his continued existence.

Where the Egyptians saw predestination, we have chance, selection, and awareness of the bifurcations inherent in dissipative structures. Where they saw cooperation with the Gods, we have sustainable development. And where they had the Pharaoh, we can have world governance. American patriots, knowing that we cannot completely master the outcomes of our acts, must cease trying to foist the worst aspects of our civilization upon the rest of the world, and show that we too have a sense of the sacred.

Epilogue:
The Case for Sacredness

The essence of natural selection is that
unstoppable tendencies of one population
to grow to the point of environmental degradation
will be halted by the growth of others. Human
population expansion plays by the same rules:
the degraded environment breeds morbidity,
high mortality and ultimately even extinction.
Lynn Margulis

The new question for science and philosophy is not what we're here *for*, but what we're here *as*. We're here as mammalian vertebrates endowed with high performance brains and nerve-jangling sensitivity. During the last ten thousand years we've come from merely staying alive to all but dominating our surroundings - only to see our survival threatened by that domination. We can produce perfect sheep from scratch, but we cannot govern ourselves.

After the discovery of quantum theory, physicists realized that they didn't really know what question the new science answered. Following much soul searching, they decided that it was enough to know that it does what it does. This marked the beginning of wisdom in the West, and quantum theory is applied to a myriad of problems simply because it works. Unfortunately, wisdom has not yet been widely disseminated. Meanwhile, thousands of years of religion have failed to help humanity find peace, and today it is overcome by the wondrous machines is has invented but cannot control. As the foreign world of representation called God ricochets back to us when we contemplate the Other, fear leads to the creation of ever more efficient means of violence. Rousseau's insistence on man's innocence is as wrong as the Jesuits' blanket condemnation, because both are based on a dualist view of reality. Instead of opposing the Other, we can accept the absence of God, realizing that the sacred is in all things: *tat tvam asi*, that art thou.

Quantum mechanics and Heisenberg's uncertainty principle do not so much contradict Cartesian logic as explicate it: 'I think therefore I am'; i.e., through cognition and autopoiesis I exist as an inherent part of the universe, not outside it as Heisenberg's observer who affects the thing being observed. Auto-referentiality is what differentiates us from plants and animals, however the flip side of that ability, as the ancient Egyptians knew, is the obligation of responsibility. There is no need to aggress the Other because his thoughts are different from ours, for even two snowflakes cannot be identical. We are both part of one consciousness, endless combinations and recombinations of indestructible cosmic particles, our internal freedom an intrinsic element in a universe impermanent in form but imperishable in its essence.

In tribal times, the Other was to be feared if unknown to friends and relatives who could settle disputes. Once reconciliation was entrusted to outside parties, men renounced the freedom to think for themselves and be responsible for their acts, deferring to external authorities. When a single all powerful God made in the image of man replaced nature Gods, every human

Other was likened to him and perceived as a potential threat. The Jews renounced their internal authority in favor of rabbis, and when that ceased to be effective, Christ offered love and forgiveness dispensed by priests, while more forthrightly, Mohammad emphasized submission to the divine will. Whatever the religion, the decision to believe in God was the most decisive act humans committed with respect to internal authority. And when they inserted the deity, an absolute, between Yin and Yang, morality identified with the oneness of life, became authority outside it, to the detriment of the Whole.

Seeing a sunset in a beautiful landscape, many people say: "There must be Someone up there for all this to exist," while others say: "How wonderful to be here, to see all this, to feel all this. There can't possibly be anyone up there. This just is." When God told Moses: "I am he who is", belief in his power transformed the unknowable into an old man in a white beard making sunsets. Knowing that although one was oppressed by one's fellow men, one had that God's love, made life - and death - easier to bear.

Marx described religion as the sigh of the oppressed creature, the sentiment of a heartless world and the soul of soulless conditions. However, it's not so much because man is repressed, as Marx and Marcuse thought, as because he has abandoned his immediate external environment that he fears death, distracting himself with Things. As he acquired ever more things, he became separated from his immediate world and from the Whole itself, and death became an intolerable prospect that proved the limits of external freedom, or the power to act.

We have no concept of freedom as part of ourselves because we do not properly value consciousness. Seen as an external good instead of an inner state, freedom is a thing we use to enjoy the world out there. Life too is a thing that we possess, but we are willing to risk it to obtain other things. Eventually we realize that things do not replace Being, but by the time we become aware of the Self as the only thing we have, it's too late. In the final humiliation of over-medicalization, which treats the self as a thing, we die unto ourselves long before we cease to breathe.

Knowing that nature is part of a Whole, we can see that God is to order/disorder what idols were to monotheism: an uninformed belief. Pantheists have always known that belief in multiple Gods leaves man's internal authority intact, and is more consistent with respect for nature than is monotheism. As Spinoza suggests, a God of the wind or rain is simply an anthropomorphic version of a scientific fact. The American Indians do not have an omnipotent God, yet they feel responsible both toward other humans and their habitat. Modern man has no concept of himself or others as part of his habitat - a modern word for 'the Whole'. Having abandoned his internal authority, and thus his individual responsibility to the closed systems built by external authority, he has no idea how to go about respecting the requirements of the open system that constitutes his environment, and includes other humans. Mind having overrun intuition, he trusts leaders to take him somewhere, but they fail because there is nowhere to go.

Modern Taoism invites each of us to participate in the life of the city, not by seeking to raise some above others, but by tending toward order. Not the conservatives' law and order, but order-in-tension-with-disorder; not rigid order that tries to impose the strongest, but Claude Jullien's order that is part of the oscillation of the Whole. Neither Jacobin absolutism that transforms tending-toward into battling-for, nor kleptocracy, which excludes participation, but an openness to all possibilities.

Once they realize that our actions are no more free than those of nature, but that our consciousness is, individuals, and groups to which authority is minimally delegated, should be able to reinvent the circular organization of life that preceded monotheism. By creating the necessary rituals at the personal, local and international level, they could accept Otherness and be with the Whole, 1 and 0, Yin and Yang, mass and energy. Quantum physics and the Egyptians' third element are not authorities outside ourselves, but an on-going process in which, through counter-balancing, what we see as alternatives are part of the same Whole.

The Egyptians had no need for a God on a throne because Ma'at, symbolizing the association between man and nature, ruled over things big and small, reasons of State and private matters. Each individual participated in the authentic reality of Being by practicing a trade in the symbolic state generated by Pharaoh. Although he did not communicate directly with the Gods, Pharaoh was man's intermediary to them, and his sacred responsibility was to administer the earth's riches for the benefit of all, through what we today call ecological management. As sole owner of the land of Egypt, Pharaoh alone knew how to respect the earth, since both were a community of elements - the Whole - fashioned by the Gods.

Technology enables us to provide humanity with all it needs, yet in a culture that attributes greater value to Having than to Being, instability becomes an uncontrollable dynamic that leads to ever more frequent and catastrophic bifurcations. To maintain a stable state, we must revive the rule of Ma'at - or cooperation with the Gods - using our inner freedom to tend toward order, while recognizing that it is inseparable from disorder. Although ancient Egypt aspired to immobility, it knew that, like perfection, immobility - or entropy - equals death. Cooperation between the Gods and man illuminates the fact that freedom cannot save the world when it is seen in opposition to death.

In the developed world, sickness is cured almost perfectly, thus unhappiness is more often related to Having than to Being, mental rather than physical. There remain unrequited love and the desire for power, but one love is followed by another, and the results of a competition are never final. Only the loss of a loved one cannot be reasoned: the pain is as deep as the joy of his or her presence, because life and death are One.

Since the Renaissance, Western culture has glorified knowledge: we do not like to see books burned, or truth obscured. But Western law and morality have concentrated on the life of only one species: man. Refusing to worship nature, they leave him free to destroy it. And yet, because we are part of a Whole which is both 'this' and 'that', no law can enable us to 'be' happy, that is to experience happiness durably. In a world that consists of enfoldings and unfoldings, there can only be moments of happiness, as well as unhappiness - pain as sharp as joy. Most of the time we experience the perpetual, indeterminate movement of the reed bending with the wind, what François Jullien calls 'the in-between'. Loving and suffering are part of the Whole which simply is. Pain is like a low cloud, the clap of thunder, but pleasures (which we are wrong to call small), are offered every day. Enjoying them may require education to the Self, not in opposition to the Other, but as part of the Whole. But to believe we can substantially transform the ego through self-help, as do Buddhists, is to deny that it is part of the order/disorder of the Whole.

Rites and temples allowed men to communicate with that which they could not see. Eventually, convinced that the invisible did not exist, they abandoned the rites and destroyed the temples. But we can only deny the Gods if we retain their message: that, as part of nature, our actions can never be totally free. Since we are one with the universe, we are one with the other. We can never find peace, because peace equals death, but understanding that the other is also entangled in the web of order/disorder, we can treat him or her with the love, tolerance and respect due each part of the Whole.

Such a transformation cannot be decreed; it must come from each of us as a manifestation of our inner freedom. When men were at the mercy of nature, they needed one or even several Gods to protect them. Now nature is at man's mercy, and only a transformation of our linear culture can enable us to understand that trying to dominate the Whole is suicidal. That we must respect the circle; that there is neither 'destiny' nor absolute God-given freedom. What we call destiny is modified at every moment by the indeterminism of life. We can only believe in ourselves, that is, in our internal authority, that is part of the Whole.

For Taoists, thinking about the speed of time or the course of events is equivalent to stepping into a windstorm that cannot be calculated. We are in that windstorm, and the more we try to hold on to the moment, the more the objects of our desire escape our grasp. If the wind were to stop blowing to enable us to grasp it, it would cease to be the wind.

Separated from the undifferentiated Whole, we have come to believe that we can dominate It. By pursuing marginal improvements *ad infinitum*, we despoil it. Politicians call for ever more growth, but if our very existence was inevitable, if we were not put here by some outside, Divine will, but are part of the Whole-that-is, then clearly, when we seek to dominate our environment, we destroy ourselves. Listen now to Stuart Kauffman:

> If science lost us our Western paradise, our place at the center of the world, children of God, with the sun cycling overhead and the birds of the air, beasts of the field, and fish of the waters placed there for our bounty, if we have been left adrift near the edge of just another humdrum galaxy, perhaps it is time to take heartened stock of our situation. We have presumed to command, based on our best knowledge and even our best intentions. We have presumed to commandeer, based on the availability of resources, renewable or not, that lay readily at hand. We do not know what we are doing. All we can do is be locally wise, even though our own best efforts will ultimately lead to our transformation to utterly unforeseeable ways of being. We can only strut and fret our hour, yet this is our own and only role in the play. We ought then play it proudly but humbly.

Evolution and self-organization tell us there are no definitive answers, and quantum theory suggests a level of reality to which we do not have access. But synchronicity reveals the identity of mind and matter, and the theory of implicate and explicate order shows that although there are no separate parts to the universe, there is always an alternative, the Egyptians' 'third element'. Embodying the sacred in each present moment, the Gods bring together opposites, what we can and cannot know.

If we worship transcendence, we cannot have faith in the inner freedom that would allow us to take on responsibilities left for too long to God, respecting Ma'at by implementing an inclusive, open politics. In its non-differenciation with respect to the other, Taoism is to the left of Judeo-Christianity, implying solidarity even when it does not try to transform tending-toward into combat. The modern Taoist has an ideal, a goal, but is able to let go when she has done what she could, knowing that the change she seeks will occur inevitably - as will just as inevitably its opposite, as part of the constant change that characterizes life.

As the only creatures who know that we know, we must not mistake knowledge for truth, for at most knowledge can bring us closer to our goals. Our education in belief, in hope as magic, rather than in reason as a moment in the process of order/disorder, hides Being, exposing us to the promises of external authority and its deceptions. Our need is for inner morality and law, to trace the limits of our external freedom.

What we cannot know is that-which-is. It is sacred and beyond understanding. When we try to control the ultimate reality of the universe, we modify it in unforeseeable ways, betraying our obligation to Ma'at. The problématique, therefore is us, and the path is both very broad and very narrow. We don't need to relive the sixties, but we do need to know that muddling through is a question of attitudes rather than rules or laws, wars or treaties. As we weigh on the endless process of life, we need to remember that disorder has neither party, sex, nor territory - and that nothing is ever final.

Glossary

System : An organic whole, which is more than the sum of its parts, and in which the modification of any element modifies the whole.

Feedback: The mechanism by which systems far from equilibrium are modified.

Bifurcation: A systemic modification brought about by runaway instability.

Catalyst: An element that has the ability to provoke change.

Auto-catalytic feedback: Change brought about by previous changes

Entropy: A systemic state in which nothing more can occur.

Equilibrium or a stable state: A systemic state which is relatively stable, headed neither to bifurcation or entropy.

Order/disorder: The alternation between entropy(maximum disorder) and dissipation which creates new order.

Dissipation: What takes places when a system becomes so unstable that it must bifurcate to another level, creating new order.

Open system: A system which is open to, or connected to, its environment. Living systems are open systems because they take in energy and reject waste into their environment.

Closed system: A system that is not connected to its environment, such as an engine.

Being: Living in awareness of belonging to the whole.

Otherness: refers to the radically other.

Having: Living to acquire ever more of the whole.

Oneness: The notion that everything is part of the same whole, another word for Unicity.

Autopoiesis: (Fritjof Capra) "A network pattern in which the function of each component is to participate in the production or transformation of other components via the circular organization of information through multiple feedback loops which constantly correct imbalances. In this process, spontaneous patterns emerge to create self organization and self-making.

Bibliography

Ariès, Philippe – Western Attitudes Towards Death, Johns Hopkins University Press, 1974

Armstrong, Karen – Islam

Arnstrong, Karen – The Battle for God

Berman, Paul - Terror and Liberalism, WW. Norton, 2003

Barrow, John D. – The Constants of Nature, Pantheon Books, 2002

Capra, Fritjof – The Web of Life

Carroll, James - Constantine's Sword

Cyrulnik, Boris – Les Nourritures Affectives, Odile Jacob, Paris, 1993

Diamond, Jared – Guns, Germs and Steel, Norton, 1997

Etzioni, A., ed. – New Communitarian Thinking, Univ. of Virginia Press 1995

Falk, Richard – A Study of Future Worlds, Free Press, 1975

Freud, Sigmund – Civilization and its Discontents, Norton, 1961

Freud, Sigmund – Moses and Monotheism,

Fukuyama, Francis – The End of History

Goldberg, Nathalie – Writing Down the Bones, Shambala, 1986

Hawkings, Stephen – The Theory of Everything, New Milennium Press, 2002

Heisenberg, W. – Physics and Philosophy

Hornung, Erik – Les Dieux de l'Egypte, Flammarion, 1991

Huxley, Aldous – The Perennial Philosophy, Harper Colophon, 1970

Ignatieff, Michael – Human Rights as Politics and Idolatry, Princeton Univ. Press, 2001

Jacq, Christian – La sagese égyptienne, Editions du Rocher, 1981

Jullien, Francois – Un sage est sans idee, Editions du Sueil, Paris, 1998

Kauffman, Stuart – At Home in the Universe, Oxford, 1995

Laszlo, Erwin – Evolution, the Grand Synthesis – Shambala, 1987

Lao Tzu – Tao Te Ching

Marcus Aurelius – Thoughts for Myself

Marcuse, Herbert – Eros and Civilization

Mishna, Pankaj - From the Ruins of Empire, 2011

McNeill, J.R. and William – The Human Web, Norton, 2003

Meadows, Dennis, L., - The Limits of Growth, Potomac, 1972

Morenz, Siegried – La religion egyptienne – Payot, 1984

Peat, F. David – Synchronicity, Bantam, 1987

Rifkin, Jeremy – The End of Work, Putnam, 1996

Scott, Andrew M. – The Dynamics of Interdependence, Chapel Hill,1982

Watts, Alan – Nature, Man and Woman, Vintage, 1991

Zukav, Gary – The Dancing Wu Li Masters, Bantam 1980